Deserted by God?

This book is provided by

TRUTHFORLIFE®
THE BIBLE-TEACHING MINISTRY OF **ALISTAIR BEGG**

At Truth For Life, our mission is to teach the Bible with clarity and relevance so that unbelievers will be converted, believers will be established, and local churches will be strengthened.

Since 1995, Truth For Life has aired a Bible-teaching broadcast on the radio, which is now distributed on over 1,600 radio outlets each day, and freely on podcast and on the Truth For Life mobile app. Additionally, a large content archive of full-length Bible-teaching sermons is available for free download at www.truthforlife.org.

Truth For Life also makes full-length Bible-teaching available on CD and DVD. These materials, and also books authored by Alistair Begg, are made available at cost, with no markup, so that price is not a barrier to those seeking a deeper understanding of God's Word.

The ministry connects with listeners at live listener and pastor events and conferences across the U.S. and Canada in cities where the radio program is heard.

Contact Truth For Life

In the U.S.:
PO Box 398000, Cleveland, OH 44139 1.888.588.7884
www.truthforlife.org   letters@truthforlife.org

In Canada:
P.O. Box 19008, Delta, BC V4L 2P8   1.877.518.7884
www.truthforlife.ca   letters@truthforlife.ca

And also at:
www.facebook.com/truthforlife   www.twitter.com/truthforlife

Deserted by God?

Sinclair B. Ferguson

THE BANNER OF TRUTH TRUST

THE BANNER OF TRUTH TRUST

3 Murrayfield Road, Edinburgh, EH12 6EL, UK

P.O. Box 621, Carlisle, PA 17013, USA

*

© Sinclair B. Ferguson 1993

Originally published in the USA by Baker Books
First published in the UK by The Banner of Truth Trust 1993
Reprinted 2002
This reset edition, using the ESV, 2013
Reprinted 2014

ISBN:
Print: 978 1 84871 153 2
Kindle: 978 1 84871 232 4
EPUB: 978 1 84871 233 1

Typeset in 11/15 Adobe Garamond Pro at
The Banner of Truth Trust, Edinburgh

Printed in the USA by
Versa Press, Inc.
East Peoria, IL

In gratitude to him who is able to keep us from falling and present us before his glorious presence without fault and with great joy

Contents

Preface

$\cdots\cdots\cdots\cdots\cdots$

The theme of this book is capable of daunting the boldest spirit for more than one reason. The subject—the sense that God has, perhaps, deserted me—is deep and in many respects mysterious. It belongs to the darker side of spiritual experience. For that reason to read about it, and indeed to write of it, can be itself a discouraging experience, laying low the spirits.

But it is, I believe, a subject of greater importance than we often care to acknowledge. More and more people, it would seem, struggle spiritually. All of us need help—how proud we are not to confess it freely! But we are not alone in the struggle, as I hope these pages will show. The psalmists are our brothers in affliction; they wrote for us. My prayer is that the consolation God has brought to many others through their words may be as real for us today as it was for them.

Books always leave their author's hands already deeply in debt! I am indebted to Allan Fisher, editorial director of Baker Book House, for first suggesting this subject to me and for his gracious encouragement and friendship. My indebtedness to my wife, Dorothy, and our children has increased with each book I have written; I am thankful for the 'overdraft' they allow me on their love and patience.

Since the focus of attention in these pages is on the Psalms, I am also inevitably indebted to the countless authors whose works on the Psalms I have read over the years. Behind that lies my increased sense of gratitude and love for those wonderful writers, the psalmists themselves. But greatest of all is the debt to Jesus Christ, who undoubtedly knew the Psalms by heart, loved them from childhood, sang them throughout his life, experienced their significance personally, and fulfilled the longings they express. My prayer is that through the particular psalms on which this book concentrates his voice will be heard saying, 'Come to me, all you who are weary and burdened, and I will give you rest.'

Sinclair B. Ferguson
Westminster Seminary
Philadelphia, Pennsylvania

Can Anyone Help Me?

Deserted by God? discusses what our forefathers in the Christian church called 'spiritual desertion', the sense of God having forgotten us that leaves us feeling isolated and directionless.

To some who pick up these pages and glance at them it may seem inconceivable that any true Christian would ever think like that. If they do, there must be something seriously wrong with their spirituality. But the conviction has gained ground in my mind that many Christians know what it is to feel at the end of their tether. To sing 'now I am happy all the day' seems to them both dishonest and trite.

Only this week I received a letter from a Christian telling me how much more difficult life has seemed since Christ took hold of her.

This book is for such Christians. It will not remove all of their difficulties; but my prayer is that it will be a helping hand on the way and will provide encouragement like a voice saying, 'I know where we are going; put your next step here and you will be able to make progress, even though it seems dark all around you.'

The format of the book—studies in the Psalms—is not accidental. Each chapter draws attention to experiences that did, or could, lead the author to feel that God had deserted him.

There are several reasons why I have chosen to write the book in this way, and I hope these will become obvious. One of them is this: we live in a world that both seeks and dispenses easy and quick answers to even deep-seated difficulties and questions. Sadly, many people are 'disappointed' with God himself if he does not provide them.

But God is not our servant; his ways are higher, deeper, broader than ours. The English poet William Cowper learned through his own deep depressions that the 'bright designs' of God are often forged in 'deep and unfathomable mines of never-failing skill.' The Psalms similarly show us how the people of God have grappled with their questions, doubts, desertions, and how God lifted them up and brought them into new light and joy.

Another important reason for approaching this subject by means of Bible study is that when we are discouraged, or face difficulties, or feel that God has deserted us, our great temptation is to turn in upon ourselves. We lose our sense of perspective, our objectivity. We need to be brought out of ourselves and have our gaze redirected from what we are and do to what God is and does. This alone will provide the reorientation we all need for spiritual health.

So these pages are biblical studies, in a sense, studies on theology as it works out in the experience of the wounded spirit.

This approach is important for several reasons. One is that in dealing with the personal difficulties and problems of others, there is a temptation for writers whose calling is to be theologians and pastors to assume that our own expertise is sufficient to deal with every difficulty. That is not the case, as our biblical and theological learning should teach us. Scripture emphasizes that we are material as well as spiritual beings and that there is constant interaction in our lives between these two aspects. Sometimes our discouragements and depressions are so integrally related to our physical condition that we need to consult a medical doctor for help and healing. It would be out of place for me to pretend to be able to give the counsel that only a trained physician can give.

But there is a further consideration. In my experience, many discouraged Christians who have sought help in their discouragement, either of a medical or a spiritual nature, have been short-changed in the counsel they have received. We are all too familiar with Christians who have been told by secular counsellors that their problem is that they read the Bible. They need to avoid it. But on the other hand, sadly, the way many Christians read the Bible and view the Christian life does in fact aggravate their difficulties.

Sometimes, secular counsellors, quite unwittingly, put their finger on a serious need many Christians have. Unfortunately they fail to provide the appropriate answer as well as distorting the nature of the problem. Their counsel is to get rid of the Bible, and the God of the Bible, when the true solution is to learn how properly to understand the Bible and to discover the God of infinite grace and compassion who speaks to us in it.

Most of us come to a book like this looking for help for ourselves or others: as quick a fix as possible. But quick counsel will only see us through from one crisis to the next. We need long-term help, and that can only be provided by long-term measures. Disciplined, thoughtful, prayerful study of God's Word, undertaken with the Spirit's help, is what we need. It will change the way we think, and consequently the way we live, and ultimately the way we feel.

This at least was the apostolic pattern. In Paul's teaching, the renewal of the mind produces the transformation of our lives and that in turn leads to a discovery of the good, perfect, and welcome will of God (*Rom.* 12:1-2).

A moving personal account by Dr John White in his book *The Masks of Melancholy* underlines this point. All the more so because he speaks from his multifaceted experiences as a qualified psychiatrist and as a well-read and widely experienced pastoral theologian.

> A second area where the pastoral counselor can offer help, whatever the root cause of the depression, is to teach and to encourage the sufferers (provided they have enough ability to concentrate) in solid, inductive Bible study, and to discourage mere devotional reading. In most depressed people devotional reading has either stopped altogether, or it has degenerated into something unhealthy and unhelpful.
>
> Years ago, when I was seriously depressed, the thing that saved my own sanity was a dry-as-dust grappling with Hosea's prophecy. I spent weeks, morning by morning, making meticulous notes, checking historical allusions in the text. Slowly I began to sense the ground under my feet growing steadily firmer. I knew without any doubt that healing was constantly springing from my struggle to grasp the meaning of the prophecy.[1]

I do not believe it is possible to overstress the importance of this principle. Of course it is unglamorous; but there is much about the Christian life that is unglamorous. The important thing is not its glamour, but that it is God's way. And because it is his way, it works.

Paul explains this in a statement we often associate with the inspiration of Scripture, although its focus is on the practical importance of Scripture in the lives of those who know and love it:

> All Scripture is breathed out by God and profitable for teaching, for reproof, for correction and for training in righteousness, that the man of God may be competent, equipped for every good work.
>
> (2 *Tim.* 3:16-17)

When we study and meditate on the Scriptures, they begin to make a significant impact on the whole of our lives. They give 'teaching'—about God, Christ, ourselves, sin, grace, and a multitude

---

[1] John White, *The Masks of Melancholy* (Downers Grove, IL: InterVarsity Press, 1982), pp. 202-3.

of other things. They thus bring us to know God, shape our thinking, and give us clear direction in life. They also 'rebuke'—searching our hearts and touching our consciences. God's word is

> living and active, sharper than any two-edged sword, piercing to the division of soul and spirit, of joints and marrow, and discerning the thoughts and intentions of the heart. And no creature is hidden from his sight, but all are naked and exposed to the eyes of him to whom we must give account.
>
> (*Heb.* 4:12-13)

A cleansing process takes place when our lives are thus exposed to the influence of God's Word in Scripture. We are, as Jesus prayed, 'sanctified' through the truth that is God's Word (*John* 17:17). That process is as important to our spiritual well-being as the cleansing of a wound is to its healing.

Paul then adds that Scripture 'corrects' us. When I was a school-boy, I regarded being rebuked and being corrected as synonymous and enjoyed neither! But Paul's word *correct* is not simply another way of telling us we have gone wrong. In fact it was used outside of the New Testament in the world of medicine for correcting a damaged limb, mending a broken leg. Through God's rebukes we see our need; through the healing powers of his Word—its encouragement, redirection, assurance—our minds and spirits can be healed.

In fact, says Paul, all the equipment to help us to be stable servants of Christ can be found in Scripture. And stability is the very quality we need when we are discouraged and have begun to think, 'I cannot stand it much longer.'

Most of all, Scripture refocuses our hearts and minds on the God whose character is revealed in it. Knowing him better is our deepest need. Meeting that need will put all of our other needs—our doubts, discouragements, depression, disconsolation—in their proper context.

On one occasion when he was greatly discouraged, Martin Luther, the sixteenth-century reformer, was forcefully reminded of this by his wife, Katharine. Seeing him unresponsive to any word of encouragement, one morning she appeared dressed in black mourning clothes. No word of explanation was forthcoming, and so Luther, who had heard nothing of a bereavement, asked her:

'Katharine, why are you dressed in mourning black?' 'Someone has died,' she replied. 'Died?' said Luther, 'I have not heard of anyone dying. Whoever can have died?' 'It seems,' his wife replied, 'that God must have died!'

Luther took the point. He, a believer, a Christian, with such a great God to call his Father, was living like a practical atheist. But Luther knew that God was not dead. God was living, reigning, active in the events of history and in Luther's own life. How foolish he had been! Discouragement was immediately banished.

Knowledge and love of God create an environment in which discouragement and a sense of depression or spiritual desertion find difficulty in breathing. That, ultimately, is what the psalmists discovered over and over again, and tell us in different contexts and a variety of ways. Let us sit at their feet and learn to see what they saw:

> Hear, O LORD, when I cry aloud;
>> be gracious to me and answer me!
> You have said, 'Seek my face.'
>> My heart says to you, 'Your face, LORD, do I seek.'
>
> I believe that I shall look upon
>> the goodness of the LORD
> in the land of the living!
> Wait for the LORD;
>> be strong and let your heart take courage;
> wait for the LORD!
>
> (*Psa.* 27:7-8, 13-14)

2

How Long, Lord?

In the summer of 1851, the lifeless body of the English missionary Allen Gardiner was found by a search party, hidden in the boat in which he had taken refuge during his last days. He and his companions had been shipwrecked on Tierra del Fuego. Eventually their remaining provisions ran out; death came slowly, but inevitably, to each of them.

We know some of the thoughts of Allen Gardiner during those days, from letters he had left for his family and from entries in his personal journal, which was found beside his body.

He was, at one stage, desperate for water; his pangs of thirst, he wrote were 'almost intolerable.' Far from home and loved ones, he died alone, isolated, weakened, physically broken. Hardly what we might think of as the end of a 'victorious Christian life.'

Psalm 13

¹How long, O LORD? Will you forget me for ever?
  How long will you hide your face from me?
²How long must I take counsel in my soul
and have sorrow in my heart all the day?
  How long shall my enemy be exalted over me?
³Consider and answer me, O LORD my God;
light up my eyes, lest I sleep the sleep of death,
  ⁴lest my enemy say, 'I have prevailed over him',
lest my foes rejoice because I am shaken.

> ⁵But I have trusted in your steadfast love;
> my heart shall rejoice in your salvation.
> ⁶I will sing to the LORD, because he has dealt bountifully
> with me.

It must have been under similar circumstances that Psalm 13 was written. It is a poignant lament. It belongs to the world of the hills and the mist and the haunting sound of the bagpipes wafting over the gloomy silence. In such songs the brokenhearted pour out their souls, and sometimes their complaints to God.

Darkness and gloom surround David. His vision is clouded. He is in a tunnel. He could cope with that if he could only see light. But he sees none. His eyes are darkened (verse 3). He cannot see where he is going, or where life is leading him. He is what Isaiah describes as 'him who walks in darkness and has no light,' who must learn to 'trust in the name of the LORD and rely on his God' (*Isa.* 50:10).

Lamentation

Two questions dominate the songs of lament in the Old Testament.

The first is 'Why?' Why has this happened to me? Why here? Why now?

The second is the question which is repeated over and over in this psalm: 'How long?' David asks it four times in the first two verses of Psalm 13. He is on the verge of despair. He sees no future. He feels he cannot cope any longer. He is at the end of his tether. Four times, with four different questions, he cries out to God, 'How long?'

At first sight the questions seem to be expressions of bitter defiance. All the more so since he actually writes them down. We modern Christians would be a little more guarded. Bad enough to think such thoughts; dangerous to put them in writing. But already David is teaching us an important lesson. He was spelling out his difficulty. His questions are actually a diagnosis of his problem. By the time he had written two verses, he had clearly stated what it was. In this case, diagnosis is half of the remedy.

There are sinister elements about discouragement. It is all-pervasive, affecting everything in our lives. Yet at the same time it is a vague generalized feeling that seems to discourage us from probing its roots too deeply lest we find the experience too painful. It is a spiritual affliction with an inbuilt immune system. As he put pen to paper, David had already begun to overcome discouragement by identifying its causes and staring it in the face: Has God forgotten me permanently? Is God hiding his face from me? Why do I wrestle with my thoughts and have sorrow in my heart every day? Why does my enemy keep on triumphing over me?

In one sense these are not four different questions, but four facets of the same great question: Why is it that I feel God has deserted me?

But do you see the importance of asking them, and writing them down? David now has something to work on. Before, he was simply fighting aimlessly in the dark.

What were his problems?

The first was this. Why is it that God seems to have forgotten me?

We sometimes speak of enjoying a sense of the presence of God in our lives. It is one of the great blessings of Christian experience. God is with us and we are conscious that he is near day by day.

David's experience was the reverse. He no longer had a sense of the presence of God, but a depressing sense of the absence of God. It felt as though God had forgotten him.

We forget someone when our real interests lie elsewhere. The person we have forgotten has lost their earlier significance to us. When we are the ones forgotten, we tend to feel rejected, passed by, humiliated. We have been made to feel small and insignificant. That clouds the way we look at ourselves and affects everything we do. It is depressing.

But to feel yourself forgotten by God is devastating, especially if you believe, as David did, that you have been made as his image to enjoy his presence.

David expresses this in his further cry, 'How long will you hide your face from me?'

Forgetfulness may be accidental: an oversight perhaps. But hiding is not; it is a deliberate act of avoidance. The God to whom David looked as the one of whose life and being he was the mirror image seemed to have turned away from him. The Lord was concealing his face from him. David felt his very existence threatened. How could life have any meaning if God turned his face away?

There was something even worse. When God hides his face, we do not know where he is looking or what he is planning.

This was David's problem: he had lost all sense of what God was doing. He could not see the smile on his face or catch a glimpse of its determined purpose of grace. He had no clues in his experience that would have encouraged him or helped him to think, 'Now I see a glimpse of what God's plan must be!'

Worse even than this, David could not see light at the end of the tunnel. He did not know if there was an end to the tunnel. God had forgotten him and hidden himself from him—*despite the fact that he had warned his people never to do that to him!* He would even later reveal himself as a God who cannot forget his people:

> Can a woman forget her nursing child,
> that she should have no compassion on the
>   son of her womb?
> Even these may forget,
> yet I will not forget you.
> Behold, I have engraved you on the palms of my hands;
> Your walls are continually before me.
>
> (*Isa.* 49:15-16).

David underlines how low his spirits had sunk. 'Will you forget me *forever?*

If the answer to the question 'How long, Lord?' is 'briefly,' or 'until this, or that happens,' we could perhaps cope. Knowing that the days of darkness will come to an end gives us enough light to help us to keep going. But David's darkness seemed to go on forever.

Our most painful experiences are like that: sorrows, burdens, disappointments that we will have to carry throughout the rest of our lives. They are irreversible.

When, for example, someone we deeply love dies, we know what David meant when he said that he had sorrow in his heart 'all the day' (verse 2). As the merciful oblivion of sleep departs from us, perhaps in the middle of the night, or as we gradually awaken in the early morning, we wonder what that vague, gnawing sense of gloom on our spirits is. Then we remember. It is another day without *him*. Now all days are days without *her*. We are overwhelmed by pain that seems to have no horizon. Can we bear it?

Lesser griefs convey a taste of this too: thwarted ambitions; the loss of a job; a broken romance; a difficult situation that cannot be resolved. Each day, sorrow fills our hearts and casts its shadow over everything we do. Will it be like this forever? We, too, ask David's question; we are no more confident than he was that we can keep going. No wonder David asks, 'How long must I take counsel in my soul?' (verse 2).

In the language of the Old Testament, 'counsel' is the activity of the mind, but 'soul' is the seat of the emotions. 'Counsel' and 'soul' do not really belong naturally together. We do not *think* with our *feelings*, but with our minds. Consequently translators have tended to modify David's words to make them seem more coherent: 'How long must I wrestle with my thoughts?' (NIV).

But perhaps the very incoherence of these words is meant to be significant. Mind and emotions are frequently confused when we find ourselves overtaken by distress and disoriented. That is part of our problem: we think with our feelings, or more accurately, we let our feelings do our thinking for us.

We recognize this in other testing experiences, particularly in relation to temptation.

Temptation appeals to the senses, the emotions, the desires. Something attracts us, and stirs up our desire to do it, or have it. Before we know where we are, our feelings are telling our minds what to think. It was like that for Eve in the Garden of Eden (*Gen.* 3:6), and for David as he was drawn into sin with Bathsheba (*2 Sam.* 11:2).

Sorrow, trials, disappointment can all work in the same way, confusing our thinking and overwhelming us. This, apparently, David experienced. He could not think his way out of his dark tunnel. His thinking was confused by his feelings.

David felt defeated: 'How long shall my enemy be exalted over me?' (verse 2). It was no longer a matter of holding out; it was a question of how long the defeat would last. He felt he had no resources left. Total despair beckoned.

We do not know who or what David's 'enemy' was. Scholars have made various suggestions. But here, as elsewhere, David is not specific.

Some have thought David was thinking about an individual, or a group, as he does later in verse 4; others have thought that the enemy here is probably death (cf. verse 3) and that the psalm was written during a near-fatal illness. Augustine thought 'the enemy' was spiritual and referred to the devil or 'the sensual habits of life.' Certainly for some of us, those, rather than other problems, cause us to despair. We feel overcome by sin, perhaps one particular sin, and feel all too little that Christ 'breaks the power of cancelled sin, He sets the prisoner free' (Charles Wesley).

David was not specific. Perhaps he wanted others to see that the lessons he learned through his experience were applicable to others whose 'enemy' was different from his own.

Light in the Tunnel

These are dark words. But we have already noticed something that David himself has not noticed. In the very act of lamenting that God has deserted him, he is at the beginning of a spiritual breakthrough.

For one thing, he is actually talking, face-to-face, to the God whom he accuses of forgetting him and hiding from him!

In addition, he specifically identifies his difficulties. While he admits that he is thinking with his feelings, the fact that *he recognizes it* indicates that a biblical mind is already at work.

There is a great deal to learn from this. Admittedly, it is easier to recognize this process in others than in ourselves. But it is vital for us to recognize what is happening here. When we begin to speak to God about the fact that he has deserted us, we are no longer at our lowest point; the tide has turned; we are on our way up again.

There are analogies to this in physical health. To know that you are ill is, generally speaking, to be nearer a cure than to be ill without knowing it. Furthermore, a patient who appears to us to be extremely ill may actually be on the road to recovery.

I recall talking with a surgeon who had operated on my mother. She had suffered a stroke in the United States and shortly afterwards was flown back to her (and my) native Scotland. But within a few days she was rushed into hospital and required lifesaving surgery for a hitherto undiagnosed condition.

Such was my mother's physical condition following the stroke that the surgeons were uncertain whether she would survive the operation; without surgery, however, she would certainly die.

Some time later one of the surgeons spoke with me. He commented vaguely on my mother's condition but then said: 'Of course, in her general condition we do not know whether she can live for seven or eight. . .' I had just seen her; I thought the last word in his sentence might be 'days.' To me she looked irrecoverably ill. My heart sank.

The surgeon finished his sentence: 'seven or eight *years*.'

I was overcome with both joy and amazement; she would live! To my untrained and inexperienced eye, her condition seemed fatal, but in actual fact she was 'on the mend.'

The same was true for David. To the untrained eye his condition seemed fatal; he thought so himself. But in fact he was already 'on the mend.' To tell God that he has deserted you; to know that you have been thinking with your emotions—these are marks of life, not of death, of hope and not of despair. Why, you are even speaking to God himself about them as though you know he cares!

Petition

What was the answer to David's sense of desertion by God? Three imperative statements tell us that he knew what it was: Consider me; Answer me; Light up my eyes (verse 3).

He had felt that God had forgotten; now he prays that God will look on him. Unheard, he asks for an answer; in darkness he still believes that God can give him light.

David's exhortation to God is more significant than it may appear to be at first glance. He seems to be consciously reflecting on the wonderful benediction that Aaron and his sons were to pronounce on the people:

> The LORD bless you and keep you;
> the LORD *make his face to shine* upon you
> and be gracious to you;
> the LORD *lift up his countenance* upon you
> and give you peace.
>
> (*Num.* 6:24-26, italics added)

In fact, what David is doing is asking God to give the blessings he has *promised*; he is urging him to be faithful to his own word, to do what he has said.

Even if we are only observers, rather than sharers, of David's experience, this is an important lesson. Learn the promises of God in advance. When the time of crisis or darkness comes, it is too late to start learning them. Store up the Word of God, like a squirrel storing up nuts for the winter; for the winter-time of life will surely come when you will need God's promises to act as an anchor for your soul.

Do you feel that God is far distant from you, and lack a sense of his presence in your life? I know a little of your experience. Here is an anchor I have often used: 'Draw near to God and he will draw near to you' (*James* 4:8). It is a promise; he will not break it. He will not resist his children's appeal, 'Father, you promised.'

Do you see what David was doing? He was thinking about God's promises with his mind, rather than concentrating on his feelings about his situation.

At last he was holding on to something outside of himself. Before, his whole attention had been fixed on the turmoil within his heart; he was looking at the storm. The storm was still around him, but now he was secured to the anchor of God's promise and was safe. Perhaps nothing in his situation had changed; but now he was beginning to know that God's promise of blessing would keep him through the storm.

He puts this another way: 'Light up my eyes, lest I sleep the sleep of death' (verse 3). He is asking here for more than the preservation of his life. He is acknowledging that while he has been surrounded by difficulties and is beset by weakness, his greatest need is not the removal of these things. They may, after all, be the means of his blessing.

Rather, David's concern is that he should have clear vision and an assured understanding of the Lord's ways with his children. He is praying for divine illumination so that he may learn to see his circumstances not with the eye of the flesh but with the vision of faith.

A remarkable example of this is found in the Apostle Paul's

experience of imprisonment. From every point of view, that seemed to be disastrous for the extension of the kingdom of God. Many of his friends were discouraged by it: 'If this is what happens to the great evangelist, what hope is there for the rest of us?' But the Lord gave light to Paul's eyes, until they sparkled with amazement and delight at what God was doing:

> I want you to know brothers, that what has happened to me has really served to advance the gospel, so that it has become known throughout the whole imperial guard and to all the rest that my imprisonment is for Christ. And most of the brothers, having become confident in the Lord by my imprisonment, are much more bold to speak the word without fear.
>
> (*Phil.* 1:12-14)

His circumstances were unchanged; he was still in prison. But his whole situation had been illumined. Now, rather than seeing his circumstances as a barrier to his service, he saw them as the God-ordained sphere for it. His imprisonment was to be an instrument of evangelism! How else could the gospel be brought to 'the imperial-guard'? They would never come to hear Paul preach; now they were compelled, as his guards, to listen to him!

This is what David prays for too: 'Lord, unless I am able to enjoy a divine perspective on my situation, I am as good as dead: Lighten my eyes!'

David adds a further concern in his appeal here. If the Lord does not help him, then his 'enemy [will] say, "I have prevailed over him,"' and 'my foes rejoice because I am shaken' (verse 4)—like a building that collapses when its foundations are shaken in an earthquake.

In most of the lament psalms some reference is made to the writer's enemies, although as we have seen, they are rarely specifically identified. They are never mentioned out of mere personal vindictiveness. They are *the enemies of God's king*. It is the kingdom God is building that they are attacking and the purposes of God they are opposing.

The same is true here in Psalm 13. David is conscious that the honour of the kingdom of God is at stake in his life. He lives in a world in which many would rejoice to see dishonour brought to God's name through the humiliation of one of his people. Hence he appeals for God to make himself known.

Recovery

Do you see what has happened? David's recovery has begun. Read again the pronouns in the opening two verses: you. . . me; you. . . me; I. . . my; my; my. . . me. He had developed an obsession, albeit understandably, with himself and his own thoughts and feelings.

But now a change has taken place. The kingdom is at stake— God's kingdom. David speaks out to God to deliver him from the enemy and to defend his divine glory. He is beginning to see light at the end of the tunnel and to lose his sense of self-absorption. Far from accusing God or forgetting him, he is now calling upon God to remember his own kingdom!

It should not surprise us that this transition took place in the context of prayer. Have you ever been so discouraged that you have had to drag yourself out of bed for a prayer time at church, or after a heavy day make a considerable effort to go to the weekly prayer meeting, or even have personal devotions? Then, as you have engaged in the work of prayer, without any conscious decision on your own part you have found yourself taken up with the needs of the church, the work of the kingdom, and the glory of God. You came weary and discouraged; you left invigorated and exultant. God was with you, and you knew it.

Something like this happened in David's life. When we read verses 5 and 6, we find David a changed man:

> But I have trusted in your steadfast love;
>> my heart shall rejoice in your salvation.
> I will sing to the LORD,
>> because he has dealt bountifully with me.

David has begun to see for himself what has already been clear to us as observers: in the process of articulating his experience of darkness, he has been giving eloquent profession to his living faith.

One proof of this is that, throughout the psalm, he has addressed God by his great covenant name, LORD. This is the name Yahweh, which God revealed to Moses at the burning bush (*Exod.* 3:13-15).

The name is significant. It is God's *covenant* name. He underlined that to Moses when he reminded him that he was the God of Abraham, Isaac, and Jacob. It is also the name whose meaning became clear in the events of the Exodus: God is a gracious and powerful, a redeeming, providing, and guiding God; a God who overcomes all opposition to his purposes.

The very God David needed, David had! So discouraged was he, however, that it took him time to realize what was always true. He even calls upon him in the most intimate way, 'O LORD (the covenant name) *my* God.' But only as the psalm ends does he begin to appreciate fully what this means. As he does so, he emerges as a transformed man. Words of sorrow yield to verbs like trust, rejoice, and sing.

What had David now remembered that he had been in danger of forgetting? He mentions three things:

1. The Lord's unfailing love brings David to 'trust,' confide, and rest in him. This is one of the Old Testament's most beautiful words. It means covenant love, the love to which God voluntarily commits himself. It is what George Adam Smith, a Scottish Old Testament scholar of a previous generation, called God's 'leal-love' (*leal* is the fine Scots word for loyalty). God is faithful. He is unfailing. Rest in him; trust him.

2. The Lord's salvation makes David's heart 'rejoice.' However great his difficulties are, he possesses something greater than them; however long they last, his salvation will outlast them.

Paul puts this in New Testament language when he writes that being justified,

> we rejoice in the hope of the glory of God. More than that, we rejoice in our sufferings, knowing that suffering produces endurance; and endurance produces character, and character produces hope.
>
> *(Rom.* 5:2b-4)

Here the apostle traces two lines that both lead to the glory of God:

Because God has promised to save those who trust in him, we learn to rejoice in our hope of sharing his glory. But in a parallel way, our sufferings create the context of persevering faith and genuine spiritual character; and that character likewise produces hope in the glory of God.

Knowing that we are already forgiven makes us rejoice; the certainty of future salvation makes us rejoice all the more. It did the same for David.

3. The Lord's goodness makes him 'sing.' To this we must return. It is a prominent feature in the psalms. God's people struggle to believe that he is good, in the face of what seems to be so much counter-evidence. But as David breaks through the clouds of gloom and near-despair that have hung over his head, he breathes the clean air of the Lord's goodness. He now sees that in all things he works for the good of those who love him, who are called according to his purpose (*Rom.* 8:28).

Allen Gardiner, with whose name this chapter began, did the same. Despite the wretched conditions in which he died, he seems to have experienced a new and deeper sense of the goodness of God. He wrote out passages from his beloved King James Bible. One of them was Psalm 34:10:

> The young lions do lack, and suffer hunger: *but they that seek the* LORD *shall not want any good thing* (italics added).

In his weakness he managed to pen one final entry in feeble handwriting into his journal. It was this: 'I am overwhelmed with a sense of the goodness of God.'

So was David.

Before we leave this brief psalm, or indeed, any psalm, there is something we should remember. Jesus must have learned by heart and sung this psalm and made it his own.

It is not difficult to see how applicable Psalm 13 would have been to Jesus during the days of his ministry. He knew what it was for life to give the impression that God had forgotten him; he had every reason to pray that his Father would protect him in the face of his enemies. He trusted in the unfailing love of his Father. He knew the deliverance and salvation of God from both enemies and death. How often he must have lain down to sleep at night thinking, 'Father, you have been good to me.'

Jesus has been where we are. He knows, he understands; he has felt it too, and he can help you. So do what Isaiah encourages you to do when he says:

> Let him who walks in darkness and has no light
> trust in the name of the LORD
> and rely on his God.
>
> (*Isa.* 50:10)

. . . .

3

Dark Valleys

F rom childhood onward, most of us are afraid of the dark. In the
dark we cannot see our way; we no longer feel in control. We
have ceased to be captains of our fate, masters of our destiny. We are
in the unknown. The last words of the short-story writer O. Henry
are said to have been the words of a popular song: 'Turn up the lights,
I don't want to go home in the dark.' Most of us sympathize with
him.

David knew what it was like to be in the dark. 'Even though I
walk through the valley of the shadow of death, I will fear no evil'
(*Psa.* 23:4).

Psalm 23

¹The Lord is my shepherd; I shall not want.
   ²He makes me lie down in green pastures.
He leads me beside still waters.
   ³He restores my soul.
He leads me in paths of righteousness
   for his name's sake.
   ⁴Even though I walk through the valley of the shadow of
death,
   I will fear no evil,
for you are with me;
   your rod and your staff,
   they comfort me.
⁵You prepare a table before me in the presence of my enemies;

> you anoint my head with oil;
>   my cup overflows.
> ⁶Surely goodness and mercy shall follow me
>   all the days of my life,
> and I shall dwell in the house of the LORD for ever.

We usually associate these words with the dark valley of mourning. Beyond all doubt they have a special significance then. For most of us that is the darkest valley of all, the one we most dread entering. But David's language is broader in scope. The valley he describes is, literally, one of deep darkness. The encouragement of his testimony is not to be confined only to the valley of death-shade; it speaks to us in every dark experience of life.

I have personally been very slow to appreciate the wisdom and encouragement of David's words. I suspect that I am not alone in this. I have to confess with some shame that Psalm 23 has been so familiar to me since childhood that in earlier life I tended to think that the only people who 'love Psalm 23' are those whose knowledge of Scripture does not extend much beyond it.

In my own case that disenchantment was increased by reading a 'child's picture-book version' of Psalm 23. The cover picture on the edition I had as a child is still fresh in my memory. David is seated on a rock, his shepherd's crook beside him. He is a beautifully complexioned, curly haired, blue-eyed boy. Nearby his perfectly white sheep graze on rich green pasture land set against a clear blue sky, whose perfection is only heightened by wisps of white cloud. All is well with the shepherd boy as he sweetly composes his psalm of praise. This is an ideal world. David lacks nothing.

Almost everything about this portrayal of Psalm 23 is misleading. Once we see that, we may be able to hear what David is really saying.

His is no ideal world, but one full of dark valleys (verse 4) and the presence of sinister enemies (verse 5). Nor is David an innocent abroad in a safe environment. He is marred, spiritually disfigured, and in danger. No inexperienced youngster this, but a man who has struggled through many difficulties to the confident faith he now confesses.

How can we share his confident faith and be as sure as he was that God will be with us in the darkness?

First we must recognize what David is doing in this psalm. Surely that is obvious? He is using his experience as a shepherd and his knowledge of sheep as a kind of object lesson, or allegory, of the Christian life. Isn't this a pastoral version of *The Pilgrim's Progress*?

In fact, David is doing something different. His starting point is not sheep and shepherding, but God's word in Scripture. He is, in fact, applying a specific passage from his Bible to his own life and saying to us: 'Let me tell you how I experienced its truth and power.'

David was not the first person to say, 'The Lord is my shepherd.' Those words were spoken first of all by Jacob. Jacob, the twister-become-prince! At the end of his life, he gave his patriarchal blessing to Joseph's sons Ephraim and Manasseh:

> The God before whom my fathers
> Abraham and Isaac walked,
> *the God who has been my shepherd all my life long to this day,*
> *the angel who has redeemed me from all evil,*
> bless the boys.
>
> (*Gen.* 48:15-16, italics added)

Here was a man who had walked through dark valleys morally, spiritually, emotionally, and physically. Brought up in a family where each parent had favoured a different son ('Isaac loved Esau. . . but Rebekah loved Jacob'—*Gen.* 25:28), he had plotted with his mother to cheat his foolish brother of his birthright (*Gen.* 25:29-34) and deceive his father (*Gen.* 27).

In a cruel twist he himself had been similarly deceived by his uncle Laban and found himself married to Leah rather than Rachel, whom he loved (*Gen.* 29:15-30). He had known fear and loneliness; but in his grace God met with him at Jabbok, wrestled with him and transformed him into a prince (*Gen.* 32:22-32; cf. *Hos.* 12:4).

But Jacob was by no means wholly changed. In later life he would imitate the mistakes of his own parents: 'Now Israel [Jacob] loved Joseph more than any other of his sons. . . And he made him a robe of many colours' (*Gen.* 37:3). The sins of the fathers appeared to be visited on the children. But God graciously 'meant it for good' (*Gen.* 50:20) as the story of Joseph marvellously illustrates.

Jacob had 'striven with God and with men' (*Gen.* 32:28). But at the end of his life he could look back and rejoice that the Lord had been his Shepherd, pursuing him like a lost sheep, rescuing him, healing him, and providing for him.

In Psalm 23, David is simply saying: 'I, too, have shared the experiences of Jacob: I too have wandered in the darkness. But what he discovered I have discovered too: "The Lord is my shepherd; I shall not want." Let me tell you what this means to me.'

When John Wesley lay dying, many of his friends came to visit him. Strong Christians as they were, they were anxious to encourage him with the promises of God. At one point, however, Wesley raised himself in the bed and with special energy said to them: 'Yes, all these promises are true. *But best of all, God is with us.*'

That is the key to what David says. He is able to look the worst of all possible situations in the face and say, 'Even though. . . I will fear [not]. . . *for you are with me*' (verse 4, italics added). He realizes that if the Lord shepherds him through the darkest valley then in every other valley in life his presence and power will be sufficient to keep hold of him.

That is why throughout so many centuries the traditional translation of Psalm 23:4, 'even though I walk through the valley of the shadow of death. . .' has meant so much to Christians. It is the Old Testament's version of the principle expounded later in Hebrews 2:14-18.

The root of all fears is the fear of death. Deal with that fear and all other fears are thereby weakened; know that the Lord will be with you then, and you will be assured that he will never leave you or forsake you. You will be able to say with Paul, 'For I am sure that neither death. . . will be able to separate us from the love of God in Christ Jesus our Lord' (*Rom.* 8:38-39).

How can we be delivered from that fear and cut off at source its ability to feed our lesser fears? The answer, according to David, lies in knowing why the shepherd's presence and his power can free us from our fear: 'for *you* are with me; *your rod and your staff*, they comfort me.' The shepherd uses the staff in his hand to work with his sheep, directing, retrieving, disciplining them; the rod or cudgel hangs from his belt, ready to defend them when they come under attack. The sheep look to these things to remind themselves that the shepherd will protect them.

David had often experienced the presence of the Lord as his shepherd protecting and saving him. Yet even David's clear view of God cannot compare with the revelation of the Lord as shepherd which is ours:

> I am the good shepherd. The good shepherd lays down his life for the sheep.
>
> (*John* 10:11)

> Now may the God of peace who brought again from the dead our Lord Jesus, the great shepherd of the sheep. . . working in us that which is pleasing in his sight, through Jesus Christ, to whom be glory for ever and ever. Amen.
>
> (*Heb.* 13:20-21)

> For the Lamb in the midst of the throne will be their shepherd, and he will guide them to springs of living water, and God will wipe away every tear from their eyes.
>
> (*Rev.* 7:17)

New Testament Christians rejoiced in knowing Christ as their Shepherd because he died their death, in their place, for their sin. Their shepherd became a sacrificial lamb, accepted by God. He brings peace to our guilty consciences. Moreover, Christ has been raised. He has conquered death. In him there is resurrection and life, which he shares with all his flock (*John* 10:10).

David glimpsed this only in outline. We see it all clearly, and our confidence in the Shepherd is all the greater. Our great enemy, death, has been shattered, irrecoverably so. Its power has been broken by Christ's victorious resurrection. Death may still take hold of us, as it once took hold of him; but it cannot keep us in its grip any more than it was 'possible for him to be held by it' (*Acts* 2:24).

We still must face death, as the last enemy. When we think about that we may tremble. But then we remember: Christ has conquered death; it may touch us, but it cannot hold on to us. Even though we walk through death's haunted valley we will fear no evil, for Christ is with us.

Christ's rod and staff are his Cross and his Word. With the first he entered into mortal combat with and defeated death; with the second he guides us through life. If these are enough to deliver us from fear and to persuade us of the Father's love for us when we are in the valley of the shadow of death, we will be able to trust him in all circumstances.

I was brought up in a small family with my father, mother, and elder brother. My mother was almost forty when I was born—by no means ancient, but certainly older than most of my friends' parents. I think partly because of that my greatest fear during childhood was the fear of losing my parents.

My parents and my brother have all died. Each died in different circumstances, and I learned of their deaths in different ways: of my father's death, moments afterward, as I arrived to visit him; of my brother's death, by means of a midnight telephone call from one of his friends; of my mother's death, as I called Scotland from a telephone in New York's John F. Kennedy Airport, en route home in the hope of being with her as she died.

Every death is a shock; terminal illness, such as my father had, or progressive deterioration, such as my mother's, are illnesses of the living, but in a vague sense 'expected.' My brother, however, died late one night without warning. I remember lying in bed hours later, so overwhelmed by the shock that I wondered whether I could sustain it sufficiently to be able to visit my mother early the next morning to break her heart with the news.

That sad journey, the words that passed between my mother and myself as we clung to each other in the valley of the shadow of death— these are the unforgettable secrets of the soul. But there is something else I cannot forget about those hours, something that sustained me then and has often done so in other circumstances since. As I lay awake, waiting for the dawn and the hour of the dreaded visit as a messenger of sorrow, some words of Scripture, lodged for many years in my memory, seemed to grow from a seed into a mighty tree under whose branches I found shelter from the storm, comfort in my sorrow, light in my darkness.

I felt those words to be true as surely as if I had heard the voice of God speak them from heaven. Here they are:

> What then shall we say to these things? If God is for us, who can be against us? He who did not spare his own Son but gave him up for us all, how will he not also with him graciously give us all things?
>
> For I am sure that neither death. . . nor things present nor things to come. . . will be able to separate us from the love of God in Christ Jesus our Lord.
>
> (*Rom.* 8:31-32,38-39)

I cannot now imagine living the Christian life on any other basis than this. If the Father loves me so much that he did not spare his own Son[1]

---

[1] Paul's verb is used in the Greek translation of the Old Testament (the Septuagint) in Genesis 22:12 in the context of Abraham's willingness to sacrifice Isaac.

but delivered him up to be crucified for me,[2] no further guarantee is needed of his wholehearted and permanent commitment to me and to my blessing.

Whatever happens to me must be seen in that light. Yes, my deepest fears may become realities. I may not be able to understand what God is doing in or to my life; he may seem to be hiding his face from me; my heart may be broken. But can I not trust the One who demonstrated his love for me? When I was helpless in my sin he sent Christ to die for me (*Rom.* 5:8). If he has done that, will he not work all things together for my good? Will he withhold any thing that is ultimately for the good of those who trust him?

In this way, Christ's death becomes the rod, the cudgel that breaks the necks of the fears that are the enemies of my peace; his word becomes the staff by which he holds on to me and rescues me from danger.

Some years ago, one of my friends had the harrowing experience of watching the life-support system, on which his teenage daughter was sustained, turned off. He and his family walked through a valley of deep darkness that we, their friends, could only observe from the higher, brighter lands. I have rarely been so conscious of seeing someone almost visibly supported by the glory of God. After the funeral he said to me, 'We know now we have nothing left to fear.' When the fear of death, the mother of all fears, is banished, other fears begin to recede.

Do you see that if he is with us in the valley of deepest darkness, we will also be able to follow David in the other great affirmations of this wonderful psalm?

Provision

If the Lord is my Shepherd, he will supply all of my needs.

---

[2] The verb is used in the Gospels of the 'handing over' of Jesus to be crucified (Matt. 26:15; 27:2, 18, 26).

'I shall not want,' David affirms. But how could he be so sure? Because of the promise of God.

David borrows vocabulary from earlier in the Old Testament when he writes, 'I shall not want.' This was the expression used in Deuteronomy 2:7 when Moses had said to the flock that God had shepherded for forty years, leading them through the wilderness: 'For the Lord your God has blessed you in all the work of your hands. He knows your going through this great wilderness. These forty years the Lord your God has been with you. *You have lacked nothing*' (italics added).

If the Lord had thus provided for such vast numbers of his people, was he not able to supply the needs of one of them?

David was confident because he also knew something about the character of God. He would supply all his needs because he was his Shepherd. Jesus helps us to understand what was on David's mind when he says that the characteristics of the good shepherd are (1) that he cares for his sheep and (2) that he knows his sheep (*John* 10:11, 14-15).

If the Lord has gone to such lengths to deliver me from death, I can be sure that he cares for me. The wounds in his hands and in his side are sufficient evidences of his love. It is beyond dispute: 'The Son of God. . . loved me and gave himself for me' (*Gal.* 2:20).

Yes, there may be times when you cry out like the disciples in the storm on the Sea of Galilee: 'Do you not care if we perish?' (*Mark* 4:38 RSV). But you cannot fix your gaze on the cross without knowing that he cares beyond words for you. If he died for you, how can you doubt that he cares for you?

Coupled with that care, however, is his knowledge. He knows you; indeed, he knows you better than you know yourself. He knows your past and your future. He knows you in depth too: your secrets, your ambitions, your fears. He knows you better than you know yourself.

This penetrating knowledge would be frightening were it not

coupled with his care. But when perfect understanding of me is wedded to perfect love for me, I can be confident of this: Whatever he sends me will bring me what I need; whatever I need, he will provide; whatever he provides comes marked with the approval of nail-pierced hands. I can trust him.

Restoration

If the Lord is my Shepherd, he will restore me when I fall.

Part of the literary beauty of Psalm 23, like the aesthetic power of a great Rembrandt painting, lies in the way in which darkness and shadow are used to highlight the beauty of the light.

Psalm 23 is full of shadows. David walks through a valley of deep and dark shadows (verse 4). Later he refers to the shadow cast on his life by his enemies (verse 5). But there is also a shadow behind these simple words: 'He restores my soul' (verse 3).

Other psalms go into considerable detail in describing the pathway that led to this quiet assurance of grace.

Perhaps David's sins and failures were so widely known when he wrote Psalm 23 that a mere allusion to them was now enough: he restores my soul. The words could easily serve as a title for Psalm 32 or Psalm 51. It may not be accidental that the verb *restore* is also one of the Old Testament's words for 'repent.'

But the picture here is expanded. The shepherd takes his sheep to quiet pastures and beside still waters in order to refresh and restore them. There is more than a word of forgiveness here; there is a sustained and prolonged treatment of grace.

David needed that! So do we. A little later we find him crying out:

> Remember your mercy, O Lord and your steadfast love,
>   for they have been from of old.
> Remember not the sins of my youth or my transgressions;
>   according to your steadfast love remember me,
> for the sake of your goodness, O Lord!

(Psa. 25:6-7)

So it is for many of us. Inexplicably, as we seek to live for Christ, we find the memories of past sin, the shame of past guilt, rekindled in our memories. Incidents, long forgotten, return; our mind is set on fire; peace and joy, praise and witness are paralyzed. We understand what Samuel Rutherford meant when he said that the old ashes of his sins became a new fire of sorrow to him. It is as though someone had penetrated our memories with a flaming arrow.

Is this the satanic attack Paul speaks about in Ephesians 6:16, the 'flaming darts of the evil one' calculated to throw our whole lives into disarray? It is certainly frighteningly alarming and spiritually destructive. But David took the shield of faith: the Lord restores my soul; he bathes me in forgiveness; he refreshes me with the assurance of his grace.

Here Jesus' description of himself as the Good Shepherd will help us. Our natural instinct is to suspect that if he restores us at all it will be grudgingly; it must be a necessary but irritating inconvenience for him.

But Christ does not come to us officiously; he comes willingly and graciously to restore us. Recall what he said to those who 'grumbled' that 'this man receives sinners':

> What man of you, having a hundred sheep, if he has lost one of them, does not leave the ninety-nine in the open-country, and go after the one that is lost, until he finds it? *And when he has found it, he lays it on his shoulders, rejoicing.* And when he comes home, he calls together his friends and neighbours, saying to them, *'Rejoice with me, for I have found my sheep that was lost.'*
>
> (*Luke* 15:4-6, italics added)

This is a parable; but the Shepherd's joy is literal. Do you really believe that?

New Direction

The Shepherd's grace is real, and free. Yet, as David goes on to stress, it does not leave us the way it finds us. Restoration leads to new direction: 'He leads me in paths of righteousness for his name's sake' (verse 3); it is restoration to following the Shepherd as Guide!

Most of the biblical teaching on guidance is summarized in this one sentence, 'He leads me in paths of righteousness for his name's sake.' The direction Christ gives us is always on the paths of *righteousness*—it involves our conformity to his word; it is *for his name's sake*—it has the glory of God, not our own ambition as its great motive.

Why this combination of grace to restore and leadership to give us guidance? Because sin produces disintegration in our lives; it causes everything to slip, eventually. Restoration is not merely forgiveness, it is transformation. We should not be deceived into thinking that the Shepherd is content with one without the other. The Lord restores us because he means to change us.

God does not condone our self-absorption. He means us to live for him, not for ourselves: 'He died for all, that those who live might no longer live for themselves but for him who for their sake died and was raised' (*2 Cor.* 5:15). The evidence of restoration is a new level of consecration.

Protection

If the Lord is my Shepherd, he will surprise me with his grace.

Many students of the psalms have been puzzled by David's words 'You prepare a table before me in the presence of my enemies' (verse 5). They have concluded that there are two different pictures being used here: the Lord is Shepherd, and we are his sheep; but he is also Host, and we are his guests.

One reason for reading the psalm this way is that presumably no ordinary shepherd would 'picnic' with his flock in wolf-infested territory!

But perhaps that is the point. This is no ordinary shepherd. His ways are not our ways; his wisdom is not our wisdom.

Can you see the sheep, gathered around the shepherd? They

hear the wolves baying, snarling, threatening. The shepherd feels the puzzled eyes of his flock staring at him, unable to understand. They had followed him gladly, trusted him implicitly, taken him at face value. Why has he brought them here? Does he not see their predicament and their fear? 'Do you not really care?' they ask.

We have heard the echo of these words above the storm on the Sea of Galilee. The disciples of Jesus found themselves in it because they had obediently followed their Master. Apparently obedience is no guarantee of a trouble-free life. 'Teacher, do you not care. . . ?' they demanded.

Our Lord rose in the boat and issued two rebukes. One was to the storm in nature, 'Peace! Be still!' The other was given to the storm in the disciples' hearts: 'Why are you so afraid? Have you still no faith?' (*Mark* 4:39-40). So long as Christ was with them they were safe until his purposes were completed. Could they not trust him even if they did not understand him? The disciples said, 'Don't you care?' Jesus said, 'Don't you trust me?'

'. . .They took him with them in the boat, just as he was' says Mark (*Mark* 4:36). Only later would they realize that he also had taken them, just as they were, spiritually impoverished, men of little faith, because he wanted to show them that they could always trust his care. It is always joined to his power.

For a moment Jesus displayed his majesty and glory; the Creator bade his creation to bow before him in silent worship.

At the time it was, no doubt, an experience they would rather have done without. But they would have been immeasurably impoverished, spiritually, if they had refused to go with him in the boat. They could never have been sure just how sovereign his control was. Now they knew!

Simon Peter, who was with Jesus in that storm, later faced one of the great crises of his life when he was arrested for preaching Christ. On the night before his trial (and certain condemnation) an angel was sent to deliver him in answer to prayer. Is it accidental that the angel of the Lord had to do to him what the disciples had earlier done to their Master—arouse him from sleep (*Acts* 12:7)?

Peter had learned that he could trust his Saviour. He was asleep like a child, secure in his presence.

Whatever trials the Lord brings us into, he means to show us his presence and glory in a way we could not otherwise learn. He knows he can keep us; but he wants us to know it too:

> Some went down to the sea in ships,
>> doing business on the great waters;
> They saw the deeds of the LORD,
>> his wondrous works in the deep.
> For he commanded and raised the stormy wind,
>> which lifted up the waves of the sea.
> They mounted up to heaven; they went down to the depths;
>> their courage melted away in their evil plight;
> They reeled and staggered like drunken men
>> and were at their wits' end.
> Then they cried to the LORD in their trouble,
>> and he delivered them from their distress.
> He made the storm be still,
>> and the waves of the sea were hushed.
> Then they were glad that the waters were quiet,
>> and he brought them to their desired haven.
> *Let them thank the LORD for his steadfast love,*
>> *for his wondrous works to the children of men!*
> Let them extol him. . .
>> and praise him.
>
> (*Psa.* 107:23-32, italics added)

Presence

If the Lord is my Shepherd, he will be with me now and for ever.

The presence of Christ with me in the valley of deepest darkness is the guarantee of his provision, of his gracious restoration, of his protection. It is also the guarantee that he will always be with me.

David reasons thus: he was with me in the valley; therefore 'I shall dwell in the house of the LORD for ever' (verse 6). Having taken us into his flock, the Shepherd gives his word that he will *never* leave us and never forsake us (*Heb.* 13:5). Never means *not now, not ever.*

David realized that this means the Lord would be with him at every stage of his life, in every situation; there and then, in glory, certainly; but also here and now. His 'goodness and mercy' (verse 6) will follow us throughout our lives; dwelling in his house will simply mean more of what we have already begun to experience.

There is a wonderful passage in C. S. Lewis's Narnia tale *The Lion, the Witch, and the Wardrobe*, when one of the children, Lucy, discovers that Aslan, the 'saviour' of Narnia, is actually a lion. Alarmed at the prospect of meeting him, she asks: 'Is he—quite safe?' and receives the reply, '"Safe?" said Mr. Beaver. . . "Who said anything about safe? Course he isn't safe. But he's good. He's the King, I tell you."' So it is with Christ. The Good Shepherd became the Lamb of God to take away the sins of the world. But he is also a lion, the Lion of the tribe of Judah (*Rev.* 5:5-6). From one point of view he does not seem safe; he does not offer us the kind of security we would choose for ourselves. We cannot tame and domesticate him to order. But he is good as well as strong; there is true security in him. He gives a peace that the world cannot give or destroy (*John* 14:27). He is good, and he is with us; that is enough.

The first physician to die of the AIDS virus in the United Kingdom was a young Christian. He had contracted it while doing medical research in Bulawayo, Zimbabwe. In the last days of his life his powers of communication failed. He struggled with increasing difficulty to express his thoughts to his wife. On one occasion she simply could not understand his message. He wrote on a note pad the letter 'J'. She ran through her mental dictionary, saying various words beginning with 'J'. None was right. Then she said, 'Jesus?'

That was the right word. He was with them. That was all either of them needed to know. That is always enough.

. . . .

4

Discouragement

Thirst, real thirst, is a terrible thing. If unrelieved, ultimately it proves fatal.

Thirst for God is often thought of as a kind of evangelical virtue, a mark of true spirituality. But we sometimes forget that the kind of thirst for God of which the Bible speaks is also a terrible experience. It means that we feel a famine of his presence, an absence of his grace and power. Spiritual thirst is painful, not pleasant; it may produce melancholy, not melody in our lives.

No more eloquent description of such spiritual melancholy exists than Psalms 42 and 43.

Psalm 42

[1]As a deer pants for flowing streams,
    so pants my soul for you, O God.
[2]My soul thirsts for God,
    for the living God.
When shall I come and appear before God?
[3]My tears have been my food
    day and night,
while they say to me all the day long,
    "Where is your God?"
[4]These things I remember,
    as I pour out my soul:
how I would go with the throng

---

and lead them in procession to the house of God
with glad shouts and songs of praise,
  a multitude keeping festival.
5Why are you cast down, O my soul,
  and why are you in turmoil within me?
Hope in God; for I shall again praise him,
  my salvation 6and my God.
My soul is cast down within me;
  therefore I remember you
from the land of Jordan and of Hermon,
  from Mount Mizar.
7Deep calls to deep
  at the roar of your waterfalls;
all your breakers and your waves
  have gone over me.
8By day the Lord commands his steadfast love,
  and at night his song is with me,
  a prayer to the God of my life.
9I say to God, my rock:
  "Why have you forgotten me?
Why do I go mourning
  because of the oppression of the enemy?"
10As with a deadly wound in my bones,
  my adversaries taunt me,
while they say to me all the day long,
  "Where is your God?"
11Why are you cast down, O my soul,
  and why are you in turmoil within me?
Hope in God; for I shall again praise him,
  my salvation and my God.

Psalm 43

1Vindicate me, O God, and defend my cause
  against an ungodly people,
from the deceitful and unjust man
  deliver me!
2For you are the God in whom I take refuge;
  why have you rejected me?
Why do I go about mourning

> because of the oppression of the enemy?
> ³Send out your light and your truth;
>   let them lead me;
> let them bring me to your holy hill
>   and to your dwelling!
> ⁴Then I will go to the altar of God,
>   to God my exceeding joy,
> and I will praise you with the lyre,
>   O God, my God.
> ⁵Why are you cast down, O my soul,
>   and why are you in turmoil within me?
> Hope in God; for I shall again praise him,
>   my salvation and my God.

These psalms belong together. In some manuscripts of the Hebrew Bible they are actually set out as one. Even in an English translation it is clear that one theme runs through them both. In fact they share the same chorus, which vividly expresses their mood:

> Why are you cast down, O my soul,
> and why are you in turmoil within me?
>   Hope in God; for I shall again praise him,
> my salvation and my God.

(Psa. 42:5, 11; 43:5)

The repetition of these words leaves us in no doubt about the theme of the psalms. The writer is 'down in the dumps.' He is struggling. He feels lifeless, badly in need of water from the springs of the living God (verse 2); he feels far away and God seems distant both in space and in time. The psalmist does not know where or when he will be in God's presence again. He is desperately thirsty.

The psalmist feels like an emaciated deer who wanders, disorientated, in search of refreshment. It cannot be found in the usual watering places; they have dried up. Its strength is ebbing; it pants, ever more wearily. At the moment its only interest in life is slaking its desperate thirst.

Soon weakness will overcome the deer, and death will come as a merciful release. But at the moment there is just enough energy left to keep on searching; nothing else matters besides water. It is a struggle just to keep going in the hope that water may be found. Inevitably the deer looks at everything in that light.

There is, this Hebrew poet tells us, a spiritual parallel: a deep sense of the absence and distance of God that drains all our energy and makes each day a superhuman effort just to get through. When we rise in the morning, we feel unrefreshed, energy-less, listless, gloomy; we see and do everything through a cloud; we live life with the shades drawn. Everything is tinged with darkness. We are downcast.

This is what the ancients called *melancholy*. The word is of Greek derivation and means, literally, 'black bile' (which the early Greek physicians believed was its cause). Psalms 42 and 43 describe a believer who has tasted it.

As a result, he has written what the titles call a *maskil*. The term comes from a verb that means 'to instruct, to make wise, to possess a skill.' Perhaps the idea is that his experience brought him wisdom and spiritual skills, which he wants to share with others.

Sometimes we go to the physician for what we call 'a complete physical.' We mean that we are being given a thorough check up; we undergo various tests to assess our physical health.

In a sense the psalms provide us with 'a complete spiritual.' Indeed, the great reformer John Calvin called the psalms 'An Anatomy of all the Parts of the Soul.' That is well put. It certainly describes what we find in Psalms 42 and 43. The psalmist speaks to us as a spiritual physician. He engages in diagnosis; he also explores the remedies that will help us.

Our Spiritual Condition

What does the physician do in order to make his diagnosis? He or she asks questions. Why? Because this will help to confirm what your symptoms are, to eliminate various possible causes, and to arrive at an accurate diagnosis.

The same is true of spiritual physicians. Skilled healers of the soul do not give counsel without first exploring the problem. That is as true when we are dealing with ourselves as when we are counselling others. We must ask, listen, analyze, and only then prescribe a remedy.

That is a difficult principle for us to learn. Perhaps the psalmist found it no easier than we do; that may explain why he resorted to writing. It took effort to analyze his condition; he was almost too weary to try. But somehow writing it out helped him. That may be worth remembering.

This psalmist is someone who talks to himself. He keeps coming back to the same question: 'Why are you cast down, O my soul, and why are you in turmoil within me?' (*Psa.* 42:5, 11; 43:5). Why 'my soul'?

To answer that question we need to know something about the way in which the Bible views human existence. We are unified persons. But we are multi-dimensional in our relations. We live in a physical world, and we ourselves are physical—we have bodies. It might even be more accurate from the Old Testament's point of view to say that we *are* bodily.

We also live in relationship to God. There is a non-bodily, non-material aspect to our existence. We are not merely biological machines; we are living persons, made for personal relationships with one another and with the God who made us as his image.

This aspect of our existence is referred to in the Bible in different ways, sometimes by the term 'spirit' and at other times by the term 'soul.' The two terms are often more or less synonymous. Mary said that her 'soul' magnified the Lord and her 'spirit' rejoiced in God her Saviour; there 'soul' and 'spirit' are complementary and almost interchangeable. But sometimes the terms denote two different aspects of our personal life. Spirit denotes power and energy (the Hebrew word for spirit, *ruach*, means 'wind in motion'). Soul, on the other hand, expresses the idea of man in his weakness and need. The Hebrew word *nephesh* sometimes seems to refer to the throat, by which man gasps for breath in order to sustain life. When it refers to the whole person, it denotes man as frail, dependent, easily bruised and broken, subject to changing moods in his experience of a fallen world. As Hans Walter Wolff puts it, the soul 'is the self of the needy life, thirsting with desire.'[1]

Ordinarily, 'spirit' and 'soul' are relatively indistinguishable. At times, however, someone whose spirit is in fellowship with the Spirit of God may experience what Charles Lamb described as 'the mumps and measles of the soul.' Everything about life may be out of sorts, even though life is centred upon God. We are like a ship, well anchored, but buffeted in the storm, tossed to and fro, here and there. The very fact that we are anchored to God, and not adrift, means that the battering we receive is all the more insistent and painful!

Sadly, Christians do not always understand. Sometimes well-meaning Christians assume that if someone is melancholic or in low spirits, the solution is all too simple and obvious. They dispense easy medicine for a disease of the soul that is difficult to cure, simple formulas that they assume will deal with every need.

But it is possible for a Christian to be seeking to walk with God, to live in faithfulness to him, and yet sense that God is distant and to be downcast in spirit.

Psalms 42 and 43 are good illustrations of this. Their author is a man of rare spiritual depth. He thirsts for God (42:2); he weeps when God is despised (42:3); he pours out his soul in prayer (42:4); God is his rock (42:9). There is not a word of confession of sin or failure in the psalm. His immediate problem is not his sin.

[1] Hans Walter Wolff, *Anthropology of the Old Testament*, trans. M. Kohl (Philadelphia, PA: Fortress, 1974), p. 25.

In fact this believer has a deep-seated desire to know the presence and will of God. That is not his problem. The issue he faces is how to deal with his discouragement as a faithful believer. The problem is not simply 'spiritual.' It is more complex than that. It involves the soul. Something has affected it. It is 'out of sorts.'

Why is it important to recognize this distinction? Because, otherwise-sensitive Christians will end up condemning themselves and feeling a deep sense of guilt for a situation in which such a response is inappropriate.

We should learn this from the way in which the psalmist addresses his soul. Similar language is used by our Lord Jesus Christ in the Gospels. Listen to him: 'Now is my soul troubled. And what shall I say?' (*John* 12:27); Jesus 'began to be greatly distressed and troubled. "My soul is very sorrowful, even to death,". . . he said' (*Mark* 14:33-34).

Do you see the point? Several temptations face us when we share the experience of the psalmist. We have seen that one is to confuse discouragement with guilt. Here is another: to think that we are alone in experiencing what we do, and that Christ does not understand. But he has been where we are—and further. He knows; he understands; he feels; he cares.

Symptoms

The psalmist's soul has been cast down. He no longer enjoys the spiritual blessings he once did. At one time, apparently, his soul had been elated, rejoicing in the Lord and delighting in his salvation (see *Psa.* 35:9). He had tasted a little of Mary's experience of joy that God brings down the proud and exalts the humble, empties the rich and fills the poor (*Luke* 1:52-53).

From those spiritual blessings he now feels dislocated. His soul is 'disturbed,' restless, lacking peace and poise. He cannot relax. He has become irritable and fretful. He has been overstretched emotionally by his experience and cannot rest.

He describes the symptoms in different ways: 'I go mourning' (*Psa.* 42:9; 43:2). His heart is heavy with grief. 'As with a deadly wound in my bones' (*Psa.* 42:10). His whole being is affected by his situation.

But his question, Why? 'Why are you downcast, O my soul?' is more important than his description of the symptoms. Only when he has discovered the reasons for his discouragements will he be able to prescribe an appropriate antidote.

We often fail precisely here. In fact, our spiritual discouragement discourages us from analyzing its causes! We yield to discouragement rather than trace back its symptoms to its root. Discouragement does not simply go away of its own account. It must be cross-examined. We must learn to say to it: 'Why are you there?' Only then will we discover that there is an appropriate medicine even for our souls.

There is help for us in studying why this psalmist experienced discouragement. He traces it to particular causes. There are specific reasons for his condition. Realizing that is half the remedy he needs.

Causes

Spiritual Deprivation

'When shall I come and appear before God?. . . I would go with the throng and lead them. . .' (*Psa.* 42:2, 4).

Weeks, perhaps months, had passed since he had worshipped with the people of God. Now his circumstances had made it impossible for him to gather with the crowds of worshippers in Jerusalem. He is exiled in Jordan, in the Hermon mountains, in the region of Mount Mizar. Here there are no songs of praise to be heard, no fellowship in which God's revelation is studied and discussed, no gatherings for prayer and instruction. Is it really surprising that his soul, spiritually undernourished as it now is, feels ground down and desolate?

Many a young Christian sitting around an open fire has been taught an object lesson by an older believer taking a live coal out of the midst of the flames, placing it apart and watching it become dim until its glow eventually fades away. That Christians need fellowship if they are to maintain their spiritual glow is the simple, but perennially important, lesson.

How important the fellowship of the church is to our well-being! Sometimes it is only when we are removed from it that we realize just how much we need it. The Lord has made us for fellowship, after all. He brought us together to need each other's love and each other's gifts.

Do not be surprised if being deprived of regular worship affects your spirits. Building individual spiritual disciplines is good; but it is no substitute for the life of the church into which you have been called.

Do not be so proud or self-sufficient as to think that you do not need regular exposure to the exposition and application of Scripture in the context of a living, praying group of Christians. Anyone who belongs to such a fellowship knows the benediction of a life punctuated by weekly seasons of worship, prayer, and biblical teaching. Not only are we thus educated in Christian truth, but our souls are nourished and strengthened. Our whole being is enriched.

When you are downcast—for whatever reason, minor or life-shaking—it takes more effort to maintain the regular disciplines of the Christian life. Even getting out to church is an enormous struggle. . . and is it really worthwhile. . . when you return home again to face your discouragements? Is it too painful for you to hear that this is the only way to sustain yourself at your present level of discouragement and not sink into worse? When these basic disciplines go, everything is in danger of collapsing—as this psalmist discovered.

Hostile Environment

'. . . they say to me continually, "Where is your God?" . . . my adversaries taunt me' (*Psa.* 42:3, 10).

He was in a distant and strange environment. That it was also a hostile one may be hinted at in the first words of the psalm if we are meant to picture the deer being pursued by hunters. It is made more explicit in what follows.

His enemies taunt and oppress him: 'Where is your God now?' they say (*Psa.* 42:3, 9, 10; 43:1-2). This was his unhappy lot 'continually' (*Psa.* 42:10). At least it felt that way to him.

We have seen before the role that 'enemies' play in the psalms. This is a conflict situation. In times of discouragement we are involved in a spiritual conflict. Under those circumstances 'enemies,' natural and supernatural, will taunt us: 'Where is *your* God?' They are often successful, for we find ourselves asking 'Where is God? Does he not care?'

Three principles will help us whenever this question arises.

1. Attack is often the best method of defence. Turn the question around on the person who asks it: 'Where is your god?' That sheds a different light on the situation. This was the approach that Elijah adopted on Mount Carmel in days when the name of the Lord was despised. He challenged the prophets of Baal: 'Where is *your* god?' and in doing so revealed their cheap taunts for the hollow words they really were (*1 Kings* 18:21).

2. Ask yourself: 'Even if I cannot sense what God is doing in my situation, and cannot understand his ways, *where would I be without him?*' To ask that question is to put things in their proper perspective. It leads to this conclusion: I can live for the Lord without fully understanding his ways; but I cannot live without him. Since he is God and I am his finite creature, he is not answerable to me; but he has proved his faithfulness over and over again. I can trust him.

3. Remember that this question was thrown at Christ too, when he was left to die in shame and loneliness on the cross: 'He trusts in God,' they said. 'Let God deliver him now if he desires him. . .' (*Matt.* 27:43).

The truth was that God was never more powerfully at work than he was in those moments; indeed Jesus knew that his Father never loved or admired him more than when darkness obliterated his conscious fellowship with heaven when he died on the cross: 'For this reason the Father loves me, because I lay down my life that I may take it up again. No-one takes it from me. . .' (*John* 10:17-18). The cross is the high point of Jesus' increase 'in favour with God' (*Luke* 2:52), even while in the darkest hour of his soul.

Jesus' soul was cast down; Jesus was distressed; Jesus had the same taunts thrown at him as the psalmist experienced. He could have stood with the psalmist, sharing a hymn book with him, and with you, as you sing this psalm. He understands, because he has been there. Your environment is not totally hostile; Christ is with you!

A Lost Role

'These things I remember. . . how I would go with the throng and *lead them* in procession to the house of God' (*Psa.* 42:4, italics added). He had been a leader among God's people and had exercised a prominent ministry. Now he was far from that sphere of ministry and leadership. It should not surprise us that he was desolated.

Few of us realise how much our sense of significance and worth is tied up with our service and leadership. We often counsel people not to become so absorbed in their service that they lose sight of the One they are supposed to be serving. But if we give ourselves in the service of Christ, who we are becomes so identified with what we do that the two are practically indistinguishable. Our service, after all, is an expression of ourselves; it is an investing of ourselves in others, for Christ. Lose that and part of our very self is lost. Discouragement is often the result.

I often think in this connection of friends who have given their lives to serving Christ overseas. They return home. There they were leaders; here they are almost aliens. There they taught, preached, pastored, made decisions; here they have no role. They find a small corner, take modest employment, have far fewer material resources than most of their contemporaries. It is easy to feel that the significant parts of life all lie in the past.

Unemployment, of various kinds, can have the same effect—whether it comes from losing one's job, or perhaps from retirement. God created us in such a way that we find significance and satisfaction in our work, as he does (*Gen.* 2:1-3, 15). To be deprived of it is to be deprived of part of our dignity. We are prevented from fulfilling one aspect of our calling—to be the image of God, to be creative and productive as he was.

The same is true in the family context: a mother gives the whole of her life to serving her family for Christ; then they leave home. For years she has sacrificed for them while many of her peers have worked and built their careers. Her husband may have done so too. She feels she has become a nobody.

The darkest cloud often comes when a mother and wife is widowed; now there is no one to serve; the struggle of the psalmist in the Hermon mountains is readily duplicated in the sitting room and the kitchen: 'Why are you cast down, my soul; why are you in turmoil? . . . I used to.' But no longer.

Notice that the psalmist's statements and questions are not simply complaints; they are a necessary reflection on his condition, an isolating of his symptoms that enables him to diagnose their causes. Once these have been identified, they can be dealt with.

So the psalmist is gradually coming to recognize not only that he is discouraged, but the reasons for that discouragement. In fact, *he has good reasons to feel discouraged;* he is experiencing isolation, opposition, and loss of position. To deny that these are reasons to be discouraged would be unhealthy psychologically and emotionally.

We sometimes distinguish between what we call 'suppression' and 'repression.' It is a helpful distinction. To 'suppress' is to recognize an emotion, anger, for example, and to master it; to 'repress' the emotion, however, is to deny that it really exists, to reinterpret it as something else. But to deny that you are discouraged or that there are reasons for the Christian to be discouraged is disastrous spiritually.

From time to time over the centuries some Christians have taught, sometimes with tragic consequences, that a truly spiritual person never gets discouraged. To be cast down is, by definition, to be 'unspiritual.' Unless we are well-grounded in Scripture, it is very easy for us to be overwhelmed, confused, and even more discouraged by such teaching.

This teaching certainly seems logical: if the gospel saves us, it must save us from discouragement! It also appears to be wonderfully spiritual. After all, are we not 'more than conquerors through him who loved us' (*Rom.* 8:37)?

But this is not biblical logic, nor is it true spirituality. The gospel saves us from death, not by removing death, but by helping us to face it in the power of Christ's victory and thus to overcome it. So, too, with sin. And similarly with discouragement. Faith in Christ does not remove all of the causes of discouragement; rather, it enables us to overcome them. We may experience discouragement; but we will not be defeated by it.

Nor is this the biblical spirituality; it is a false 'super-spirituality' that ignores or denies the reality of our humanity. We live in frail flesh and blood and in a fallen world which, John says, 'lies in the power of the evil one' (*1 John* 5:19). There is much to discourage. Jesus felt that. To be free from the possibility of discouragements would be more 'spiritual' than Jesus—and therefore not truly spiritual at all.

Psalms 42 and 43 teach us the biblical approach to discouragement: we feel it, we recognize it for what it is, and we analyze the reasons for its presence.

There were very real and painful reasons for the psalmist's discouragements. He identifies them. *But then he prescribes the divine antidote!*

The Remedy

The biblical remedy can be simply stated. It is true that there are reasons for being discouraged; *but there are better and stronger reasons for being encouraged.*

Earlier the psalmist had made the mistake of allowing his discouragements to dictate his mood while all other voices (particularly God's and his own!) had been forced to listen. Now it dawns on him that discouragements have no right to speak the last word. He begins to speak.

He talks to his discouraged soul. He preaches to it, bringing it under the authority of God's word and will for his life. He also talks to God about his needs. He even talks about the future, which had been completely obscured from his thinking all the time the voice of discouragement had been dominant.

There are three parts to this remedy. The psalmist discovered it by trial and error. By sharing it he puts us in the stronger position of knowing it in advance of the onslaught of discouragement in our own lives.

Thinking

He refocuses his thinking. His soul is discouraged and downcast. In asking 'Why?' (*Psa.* 42:5, 11; 43:5) he is not suggesting that his discouragement is unreal, but that it is not ultimately invincible for the one whose hope is in God: 'Hope in God; for I shall again praise him.'

'Hope' in Scripture is not wishful thinking. It is confidence based on the promise of God; it is the assurance that we will experience blessings we do not yet experience. That certainty is based on the fact that he is 'my Saviour and my God.'

In fact, as our author has written his way through his experience, even at his most melancholy, this has always been true for him.

He has known God as 'the living God' (*Psa.* 42:2); out of the depths of his soul he has responded to the echoes in nature of God's majesty and power: 'Deep calls to deep at the roar of your waterfalls' (*Psa.* 42:7). All nature displays his glory: the waterfalls are his. Even the 'breakers' and 'waves' which 'have gone over me' are 'yours' (*Psa.* 42:7).

God is still in control of the providences in which the psalmist finds himself. He has promised to work all things together for the good of those who love him and have been called according to his purpose (*Rom.* 8:28). There is no need for despair.

He has known the Lord as 'God my rock,' even when he was protesting, 'Why have you forgotten me? Why. . .' (*Psa.* 42:9). When he feels 'rejected' it is by 'the God in whom I take refuge' (*Psa.* 43:2)!

'Soul,' he says to himself, 'have you forgotten who your God is? He is great and glorious—a Saviour, a Living Lord, a Rock, a Stronghold. Why are you cast down? Hope in him!'

Praying

He refocuses his prayers. One of the noticeable features about these psalms is that their tone changes with the words 'Send out your light and your truth' (*Psa.* 43:3). Beforehand there is complaint intermingled with a strenuous effort to bring encouragement ('Why are you cast down. . .?'). His attention has been largely on himself and his own needs. In one sense even his self-exhortation has been in-turned. Now, however, he asks God to shed light on his darkness and reveal truth to his confused mind.

Ever since creation, light has been brought to God's people by God's living Word: 'The unfolding of your words gives light; it imparts understanding to the simple' says another psalm (*Psa.* 119:130).

But does this work? A mind well stocked with the knowledge of Scripture is a great preservative from overmuch discouragement; it is like a well-stocked pharmacy in which remedies are always at hand.

But in addition this involves making sure that our lives are exposed to a consistent biblical ministry in which the truth and power of God's word are surrounded by prayer. The exposition of God's word ('the unfolding of your words') will then do its own encouraging work in us.

This point cannot really be over-emphasized today. It is widely recognized that our own times scorn thinking and emphasize feeling. Sadly, the litmus test of a worship service is often whether or not it makes us feel good, not whether it is centred on the Lord (What would Isaiah have made of that?). But discouraged Christians need much more than an emotional pick-me-up. They need light that will dispel the darkness.

The 'unfolding' of God's words normally requires patience and discipline. But through it we are 'built up,' made more secure, less liable to easy discouragement.

It is clear that this was the case with the psalmist. Even in his discouragement he is saved from being overwhelmed, by the knowledge of God he had received in the past from his Word. Even at his lowest ebb he knew God as Saviour, Living God, Rock, and Stronghold. Now he is praying that the light that radiates from these great biblical truths about God would flood his soul and dispel his discouragement. For him, as for the apostles, prayer and the ministry of the word went together (*Acts* 6:4). He is proving for himself that this is the long-term answer to the discouragements he feels.

Seeing

He refocuses his vision. He has looked within; he has looked around; slowly he has begun to look upward and outward. Now he begins to look to the future: 'I will go to the altar. . . I will praise you' (*Psa.* 43:4).

When we allow discouragement to dictate the conversation, we look inward, downward, and backward. When God's word dictates it, we look upward, outward—yes, and forward.

Discouragement tells us we dare not think of the future, and thus obscures from us the blessing that God has promised to give to us in it. At best, discouragement allows us to glimpse the future only in the dim light of the present. But God's word encourages us to look at the present in the bright light of the future. Then we see that present discouragements are not worth comparing with future encouragements (*Rom.* 8:18), and that our light affliction is the pathway to glory (*2 Cor.* 4:17).

For to his altar I will go, 'to God my exceeding joy' (*Psa.* 43:4).

Where are discouragements now?

And so these psalms end with the same refrain. The words are the same, but the tone is altogether different. The question now is not an expression of the soul's troubles but of its triumph:

> Why are you cast down, O my soul,
>   and why are you in turmoil within me?
> Hope in God; for I shall again praise him,
>   my salvation and my God.
>
> (*Psa.* 43:5)

Like the psalmist we may have good reason to feel discouraged and to thirst for the presence of God. But we have an even better reason to be encouraged. We know that Jesus Christ has come to share the deep discouragements of a fallen world. We remember his cry on the cross, 'I thirst,' (*John* 19:28) as he sensed himself far distant from the presence and fellowship of God.

It is precisely because he tasted that spiritual desolation that we need not: 'whoever drinks of the water that I give him will never be thirsty again. The water that I will give him will become in him a spring of water welling up to eternal life' (*John* 4:14).

5

. . . .

My Sin

Catherine the Great is reputed to have said, 'The good Lord will forgive, that is his business.' She could not have given clearer evidence that she knew very little about forgiveness. It was not forgiveness she wanted; she did not really think she needed it.

The prophets knew better: 'your iniquities have made a separation between you and your God, and your sins have hidden his face from you. . .', says Isaiah (*Isa.* 59:2). Jeremiah speaks in the same vein: '. . . your sins have kept good from you' (*Jer.* 5:25).

There are many reasons why we feel the absence of the presence of God. We suspect that God has distanced himself from us; we have lost the sense of his presence and the assurance of his grace. We fear it may be because we have sinned.

That is not always so, but what if, on this occasion, we are right? What if our sin has hidden his face from our sight and deprived us of the good things of his presence?

To what psalm shall we now turn? The more serious the question, the more obvious the answer: to the psalm that begins, 'Have mercy on me, O God. . . Against you, you only, have I sinned. . .' (*Psa.* 51:1, 4). David has written this psalm specially for us: 'I will teach transgressors your ways, and sinners will return to you' (*Psa.* 51:13). How can we learn to find our way back into God's presence when we have sinned?

Psalm 51

[1]Have mercy on me, O God,
 according to your steadfast love;
according to your abundant mercy
 blot out my transgressions.
[2]Wash me thoroughly from my iniquity,
 and cleanse me from my sin!
[3]For I know my transgressions,
 and my sin is ever before me.
[4]Against you, you only, have I sinned
 and done what is evil in your sight,
so that you may be justified in your words
 and blameless in your judgement.
[5]Behold, I was brought forth in iniquity,
 and in sin did my mother conceive me.
[6]Behold, you delight in truth in the inward being,
 and you teach me wisdom in the secret heart.
[7]Purge me with hyssop, and I shall be clean;
 wash me, and I shall be whiter than snow.
[8]Let me hear joy and gladness;
 let the bones that you have broken rejoice.
[9]Hide your face from my sins,
 and blot out all my iniquities.
[10]Create in me a clean heart, O God,
 and renew a right spirit within me.
[11]Cast me not away from your presence,
 and take not your Holy Spirit from me.
[12]Restore to me the joy of your salvation,
 and uphold me with a willing spirit.
[13]Then I will teach transgressors your ways,
 and sinners will return to you.
[14]Deliver me from bloodguiltiness, O God,
 O God of my salvation,
 and my tongue will sing aloud of your righteousness.
[15]O Lord, open my lips,
 and my mouth will declare your praise.
[16]For you will not delight in sacrifice, or I would give it;
 you will not be pleased with a burnt offering.
[17]The sacrifices of God are a broken spirit;

> a broken and contrite heart, O God, you will not despise.
> ¹⁸Do good to Zion in your good pleasure;
>   build up the walls of Jerusalem;
> ¹⁹then will you delight in right sacrifices,
>   in burnt offerings and whole burnt offerings;
>   then bulls will be offered on your altar.

The title of the psalm gives us immediate encouragement. It was composed after David was exposed for the sins of adultery with Bathsheba and complicity in the planned homicide of her husband, Uriah the Hittite (*2 Sam.* 11-12). He had nowhere to hide, no excuses. To a degree that he had never experienced before, he now knew that he was a sinner.

Yet, David experienced forgiveness. He discovered:

> Blessed is the one whose
>   transgression is forgiven, whose sin is covered.
> Blessed is the man against whom
>   the LORD counts no iniquity.
>
> *(Psa.* 32:1-2)

We can discover that too, if we will let David be our teacher, as he requested.

I Have Sinned

We have already noticed that discouragement tends to paralyze our ability to explore its causes. Sin has a similar effect on us; it desensitizes us to its true nature and blinds us to its significance. In that hardened condition, the last thing David was likely to do was to examine himself and his sin. But until he did he could not taste the blessings of forgiveness.

Nathan the prophet was the brave instrument who awakened David out of his spiritual lethargy. Nathan made David think about his sinfulness: 'Why have you despised the word of the LORD, to

do what is evil in his sight?. . . you have despised me. . .' (2 *Sam.*
12:9-10).

The Nature of Sin

God has many instruments to serve as prophets through which
light dawns on us and we see ourselves as we really are. As with
David, it may be through a sermon God speaks to us; or, like Jonah,
through painful providences by which he touches our lives and awak-
ens our consciences. We may be arrested by the Christ-likeness of
someone else and realize how far short we fall in our own lives. The
specific instrument is less important than its effect—bringing us to
say, 'Lord, I have sinned against you.'

What stands out in David's confession is his excruciating discovery of what was really in his heart. There were layers of sin
in his soul, or, to change the metaphor, peaks of evil, which rose
one beyond the other, another becoming visible only when one
had been scaled. He ransacks the Old Testament vocabulary as
he explores his soul and provides a series of vivid word pictures
to describe his need.

'*My transgressions*' (verse 1) suggests rebellion and self-assertive-
ness. He makes himself the centre of the universe and his heart is
antagonistic to any rival for its throne even when that rival is a loving
Creator.

'*My iniquity*' (verse 2) conveys the idea of a twisted wayward-
ness that vitiates our lives; the fatal flaw that destroys everything.
Paul speaks about sinful man 'exchanging' the glory of God (*Rom.*
1:23). That is the fatal mistake. Go wrong here and everything
about me is wrong. Made to glorify God and enjoy him forever,
I seek to glorify myself, twist and pervert my purpose, and in the
end enjoy nothing forever.

'*My sin*' (verses 2-3) denotes his failure. David has missed the
mark, deviated from the goal for which he was created. Not only

was he made to live for God's glory but to reflect that glory. He has squandered his destiny.

'*What is evil*' (verse 4). Here is the shocking truth he has discovered about himself: he has done evil, and that evil is the fruit of an evil heart.

Nothing is more characteristic of us than the easy assumption that we are by nature basically good; that we sin despite ourselves. A covetous, hateful or immoral thought? We see them as aberrations. But David has been confronted (and confronts us) with the ego-shaking truth: that is what he is really like.

In a famous passage in his *Confessions*, Augustine tells how as a youngster he enjoyed stealing pears from a local orchard. As he looks back upon those days of supposed innocence he analyzes his motives. Why, when he had honest access to better pears, did he take those to which he had no right? He stole, he concludes, for the sake of stealing; he sinned because he loved sin rather than God.

Stolen fruit tastes the sweetest—or so we foolishly imagine, all the while protesting, 'But you could hardly call that stealing, could you?' Bank robbery, that is covetousness and theft; but David's adulterous thoughts, and then his adultery—when Bathsheba was willing? 'Yes, theft it is,' proclaimed the brave and good Nathan. 'You stole what belonged to another. You are a thief, an adulterer, and a murderer, *King* David.'

What happens when we are finally convinced of our need for forgiveness? We begin to face up to the real nature of sin. We call it by its proper names: transgression, iniquity, sin, evil.

We also begin to use the first person singular: 'my': *my* transgressions, *my* iniquity, *my* sin, *my* evil. It is not someone else's fault, nor the fault of my circumstances. It is my fault. Like prodigal sons we cry out, 'I have sinned against heaven and before you. I am no longer worthy. . .' (*Luke* 15:21). We use avoidance language no longer. Sin is sin, and this sin is mine.

This is a necessary, but excruciating self-discovery. David confesses that what God desires, he lacks: 'truth in the inward being' (verse 6).

Nor is this a recent failure: 'Behold, I was brought forth in iniquity and in sin did my mother conceive me' (verse 5), he confesses. David is not using yet another avoidance tactic here; he is recognizing that his sinfulness is ineradicably deep, woven into the warp and woof of his being, inextricably intertwined with his existence. The deformity is congenital, as deep as his bearing of the family likeness. He is inescapably sinful. Its grip on him is unbreakable.

Nathan leaves the royal presence, and the king's servants are dismissed one by one, leaving David alone in his chamber. Can you not hear him say: 'Oh, God: Is this what I have become? Is this what I really am?'

If you have never cried out like that, it is unlikely that you have tasted the depths of forgiveness about which the Bible speaks.

Have you hidden (Pharisee-like, although you would despise them) behind the fact that outwardly you have not seriously breached the law of God? But, if Jesus' teaching is to be trusted, inwardly you have broken every commandment.

Remember Isaiah's *cri du coeur* when he encountered God exalted in his holiness? 'I am undone.' He was staggered and shattered by the discovery of the truth about himself (*Isa.* 6:5).

Imagine for a moment that the prophet had made his way, later in the day, to a friend's house to seek counsel and encouragement. 'I realize now that I am a man of unclean lips,' he tells his friend. What would we moderns say to him? Would we encourage him as we do ourselves by saying: 'Isaiah, you're not that bad; in fact you have surpassed us all in holiness; God has given you wonderful lips—you are a greatly gifted preacher.' I suspect we would, alas.

But Isaiah had seen the devastating, shattering truth about himself. It was not in his weaknesses, but in his strengths, in his spiritual gifts, that his sin was subtly and inextricably intertwined. He was simply speaking the truth. His lips were contaminated.

Only those who have come to that self-discovery will be prepared to experience the live coal that brings forgiveness. It comes from the altar of God. It burns. But it burns us clean (see *Isa.* 6:6-7).

Effects of Sin

The great temptation for us as modern Christians is to believe that the quicker we can get on with things the better. If we have a sense that God is far from us, the quickest route to removing that discomfort is the one we normally seek and take. But shortcuts in spiritual things are always a prelude to disaster.

One of the marks of a deep work of grace in David's life was that he wanted to teach transgressors that God's ways are often slower, yet deeper and wiser, than ours. Not content with his recognition of the nature of sin, he now teaches us what its effects and consequences are.

Sin brings guilt. We rightly distinguish between guilt and guilt feelings. It is possible to experience the latter, yet not to have the former, and *vice versa*. We need to distinguish between these two things.

David realized that. Here he tells us that he was haunted by feelings of guilt: 'For I know my transgressions, and my sin is ever before me' (verse 3). He is like Lady Macbeth in Shakespeare's great play *Macbeth*. Guilt feelings pursue her night and day following her murderous act:

> Out damnèd spot. . .
> Here's the smell of the blood still:
> All the perfumes of Arabia
> will not sweeten this little hand.

Earlier, David knew none of this. His heart had been hardened by the deceitfulness of sin before God spoke to him. Then his defences were pierced, and the flood of guilt feelings that followed was uncontrollable. With good reason: *he was profoundly guilty.*

That is why his cry is not: 'Make me feel better; I don't like feeling guilty.' It was: 'I am guilty; have mercy on me!'

Only the latter cry will bring us true peace.

Sin creates defilement. David saw that the sin in his heart was multi-faceted ('transgression,' 'iniquity,' 'sin,' 'evil'). He also recognized how deeply its defilement penetrated into his soul. His cries for a divine remedy underline this. He uses three more vivid word pictures.

He feels as though the record of his sins had been written down on a clay tablet. 'Blot out my transgressions' he cries; break the tablet on which they have been written; destroy the record of my guilt, for 'If you, O LORD, should mark iniquities, O Lord, who could stand?' (*Psa.* 130:3).

He sees the guilt of his sin as a deep, virtually indelible dye on his character. 'Wash me thoroughly from my iniquity,' he pleads. He uses an intensive expression. He needs multiple washings to be clean.

We are too familiar with modern conveniences to grasp this picture immediately. When I was a little boy we had no washing machine in our home; my mother washed all our clothes by hand. I can picture her now scrubbing the dirt out of my soccer clothes with the help of a 'scrubbing board' covered in rounded metal ridges. It was arduous work, manually washing away the ingrained dirt.

We cannot effect such a vigorous washing of ourselves, as Jeremiah points out:

'Though you wash yourself with lye and use much soap, the stain of your guilt is still before me, declares the Lord GOD.' (*Jer.* 2:22). God alone can do the washing.

That is what David is talking about. He is asking God to scrub his heart until the defilement of his guilt is washed away.

Then he prays, 'Cleanse me from my sin.' This is the language of purgation and purification. It reappears in Malachi's description of God purging his people:

But who can endure the day of his coming? Who can stand

when he appears? For he will be like a refiner's fire or a launderer's soap. He will sit as a refiner and purifier of silver; he will purify the Levites and refine them like gold and silver.

(*Mal.* 3:2-3 NIV)

Nothing less will suffice to cleanse our conscience from guilt.

Sin causes spiritual helplessness. It makes us unstable. Hence David prays for 'a steadfast spirit' (verse 10, NIV). Sin makes us unreliable and foolish; hence he must pray to be taught 'wisdom in the secret heart' (verse 6).

His sinful heart had deceived and driven him into thoughts, plans, and actions marked by complete folly.

It always does. 'The heart is deceitful above all things and desperately sick; who can understand it?' (*Jer.* 17:9). When we follow it, we begin to think that God does not see our thoughts and acts; or that he does not care; or that it will not have serious consequences; or that it does not matter.

James describes the reality of the situation in words that provide a spiritual commentary on David's life at this point:

> But each person is tempted when he is lured and enticed by his own desire.
> [*It was not God, nor Bathsheba, but David who bore the responsibility; he should have left the palace rooftop and prayed to be protected from his own lusts.*]
> Then desire when it has conceived gives birth to sin,
> [*Spiritual adultery in David's case involved physical adultery.*]
> and sin when it is fully grown
> [*Lust led David into adultery, adultery into murder.*]
> brings forth death.
> [*The baby Bathsheba conceived died. A tragic reminder of David's spiritual condition.*]

(*James* 1:14-15)

It is hardly surprising that James's next words are: 'Do not be deceived, my beloved brothers' (*James* 1:16).

Out of his newly awakened sense of need David calls upon God to do something new: 'Create in me a clean heart, O God' (verse 10). The verb he uses occurs originally in the creation narrative in the first chapter of Genesis. God is always its subject. It describes the act of creation he alone can perform. Only God can change him, David is admitting; only God can make him pure; only God can make his heart obedient.

Only God can save a helpless sinner; only God can save me. Otherwise I am hopelessly, helplessly and permanently lost. We are driven to sing in the spirit Augustus Toplady teaches us in his hymn 'Rock of Ages':

> Guilty, vile and helpless we. . .
> Nothing in my hands I bring. . .
> Naked come to Thee for dress;
> Helpless look to Thee for grace. . .
> Thou must save, and Thou alone.

How does that strike you?

Sin brings us into danger. David recognizes this when he asks to be saved from 'bloodguiltiness' (verse 14), or 'deadly guilt.' He feels this intensely. He cannot bear to know that God is looking at him—'Hide your face from my sins,' (verse 9)—yet he fears even more lest God should 'cast me from your presence' (verse 11, NIV).

God exposes what we endeavour to conceal. Everything lies before him like an open book. There is no hiding place from his judgment. David fears that God will cast him into the outer darkness, out of his presence (verse 11). The Aaronic blessing will never again be pronounced on him. The sense of the absence of God will be permanent.

No wonder it seems as though the sound of 'joy and gladness' (verse 8) will never be heard again. His sin has made him liable to the danger of the wrath of God. And he knows that he has no defence:

> Against you, you only, have I sinned
> and done what is evil in your sight,
> so that you may be justified in your words
> and blameless in your judgement (verse 4).

Before God every mouth is shut; we are guilty. There is nowhere in the universe to hide. This is the effect of sin.

Is there, then, no hope for David, and no hope for me either? Thankfully he discovered that there is.

Forgiveness

'I deserve to be forsaken by God' is David's confession.

He is justified when he issues his judgment of condemnation; absolutely justified (verse 4). We cannot appeal to the quality of our lives, our good deeds, our spirituality, nor to the justice of God, for salvation. On all of these counts the righteousness of his condemnation of us would simply be confirmed.

How, then, can David rediscover the presence of God, hear joy and gladness (verse 8) and have the joy of his salvation restored to him (verse 12)? There is only one hope. He throws himself upon the absolutely unmerited mercy of God:

> Have mercy on me. . .
> your steadfast love
> your abundant mercy
> blot out. . .
> Wash me thoroughly. . .
> cleanse me.

Here again the language is vivid. Mercy is related to the Hebrew word for a mother's womb. It is as though David were issuing an appeal to his Creator based on the fact that he had been formed, nourished, and preserved by him throughout life.

Perhaps the child that Bathsheba had borne was now dead. Was David freshly sensitive to the love that a mother has for the child of her womb? Was he appealing, desperately, to whatever it is in the heart of God that is reflected in the unique love of a mother as she listens to her helpless infant's incoherent cries? Will God not hear the cry of a heart that is crushed and broken?

There is one final court of appeal, beyond God's mercy, greater even than his 'abundant mercy.' It is God's 'steadfast love' (verse 1).

The word David uses is 'covenant-love' (*chesedh*). It is the love to which God has committed himself, even obligated himself, in his covenant promise to his people.

It is as though David were saying: 'O God, obligate yourself to love me with a love that will save me from my guilt.' He scarcely knew what he was asking for.

Do we, when we ask for the forgiveness of sins?

In asking for 'mercy,' David, you are asking that God will show it to you, but withdraw it from Jesus.

In asking to experience God's 'steadfast love,' you are asking that Jesus will feel it has been removed.

In asking to taste God's 'abundant mercy,' you are asking him to refuse it to Jesus as he dies on the cross.

In asking God to 'blot out' your transgressions, you are asking that they will be obliterated by the blood of Jesus.

In asking to be washed, you are asking that the filth of your sin will overwhelm Jesus like a flood.

In asking to know the joy of salvation, you are asking that Jesus will be a Man of Sorrows, acquainted with grief.

In asking to be saved from bloodguiltiness, you are asking that in your place Jesus will be treated as though he were guilty.

In asking that your lips will be opened in praise, you are asking that Jesus will be silenced, as a sheep before her shearers is silent.

In asking that the sacrifice of a broken spirit, a broken and contrite heart be acceptable, you are asking that Jesus' heart and spirit will be broken.

In asking that God will hide his face from your sins, you are asking that he will hide his face from Jesus.

In asking that you will not be cast out of God's presence, you are asking that Jesus will be cast out into outer darkness instead.

Is that what we want? It is the only thing that will prevent a sense of the absence of God from becoming permanent in our life. But dare we ask God to do this for us? To obligate himself to love us in such a manner as this?

We do not need to ask him. He has already done it. In Christ he has already done everything that is necessary for our salvation. Now all we need is Christ. In him we see the Father (*John* 14:9). In his face the glory of God, obscured by our sin, has become visible again. In him there is redemption, the forgiveness of our sins (*Eph.* 1:7).

During the American War of Independence an English soldier, Major John André, was captured and condemned to death as a spy. His personal character left an indelible impression on everyone who met him while he awaited his execution. When he heard that the sentence had been carried out George Washington himself wrote that 'while we yielded to the necessity of rigor, we could not but lament.' It was only after his execution that the deepest explanation for his poise was discovered—in the following poem found in his pocket:

The Hiding Place

Hail, sovereign love that first began
    The scheme to rescue fallen man!
Hail, matchless free, eternal grace
    That gave my soul a hiding place.

Against the God who rules the sky
    I fought with hand uplifted high;
Despised the notion of his grace
    Too proud to seek a hiding place.

Enwrapt in thick Egyptian night,
    And fond of darkness more than light,
Madly I ran the sinful race,
    Secure without a hiding place.

And thus the eternal counsel ran:
    'Almighty love, arrest that man!'
I felt the arrows of distress,
    And found I had no hiding place.

Indignant Justice stood in view;
    To Sinai's fiery mount I flew;
But Justice cried, with frowning face,
    This mountain is no hiding place.

E'er long a heavenly voice I heard
    And Mercy's angel form appeared;
She led me on with placid pace,
    To Jesus as my hiding place.

Should storms of sevenfold thunder roll,
    And shake the globe from pole to pole;
No flaming bolt could daunt my face,
    For Jesus is my hiding place.

On him almighty vengeance fell,
    That would have sunk a world to hell;
He bore it for the chosen race,
    And thus became their hiding place.

A few more rolling suns at most
    Will land me on fair Canaan's coast;
Where I shall sing the song of grace,
    And see my glorious Hiding Place.

That is but an echo of what David wrote in Psalm 32, traditionally read as a later reflection on the sin described in Psalm 51:

You are a hiding place for me;
you preserve me from trouble;
you surround me with shouts of deliverance.

(Psa. 32:7)

6

. . . .

No Escape?

I am sitting in a great cathedral in England; angelic-faced choirboys stand in their places as the anthem begins. In the English manner, advance notice of the title of the anthem (but not of the sermon!) has already been published in the Saturday morning edition of *The Times*. Anticipation becomes reality as a boy soprano's voice pierces the air:

> Oh, for the wings
> For the wings of a dove. . .

The words carry to every corner of the magnificent ancient building and seem to bathe my whole being in an other-worldly atmosphere of tranquillity. I feast on the emotional richness of the experience. But then I hear another less welcome sound—my radio alarm. It is time to get up. I turn over in bed. Why do I feel a weight on my spirits, a sadness that is more than disappointment that the cathedral choir was only a dream? Then I remember. 'Today is. . .' and the anguished rather than melodious cry of the psalmist comes back to me:

> Oh, that I had wings like a dove!
>   I would fly away and be at rest;
> Yes, I would wander far away;
>   I would lodge in the wilderness;
> I would hurry to find a shelter
>   from the raging wind and tempest.

> (*Psa.* 55:6-8)

What is it that I cannot face, that makes me want to escape?

It could be almost anything. It could be the prospect of meeting someone whom you dread seeing. It may be the prospect of another day without seeing someone you feel you cannot live without. For you, Psalm 55 is not a beautiful aria but a desperately painful reality. You also long to escape. Any desert would suffice, so long as it provided relief.

In your heart you know, however, that there is no escape even in the desert.

Psalm 55

¹Give ear to my prayer, O God,
  and hide not yourself from my plea for mercy!
²Attend to me, and answer me;
  I am restless in my complaint and I moan,
because of the noise of the enemy,
  because of the oppression of the wicked.
³For they drop trouble upon me,
  and in anger they bear a grudge against me.
⁴My heart is in anguish within me;
  the terrors of death have fallen upon me.
⁵Fear and trembling come upon me,
  and horror overwhelms me.
⁶And I say, 'Oh, that I had wings like a dove!
  I would fly away and be at rest;
⁷yes, I would wander far away;
  I would lodge in the wilderness; *Selah*
⁸I would hurry to find a shelter
  from the raging wind and tempest.'
⁹Destroy, O Lord, divide their tongues;
  for I see violence and strife in the city.
¹⁰Day and night they go round it
  on its walls,
and iniquity and trouble are within it;
    ¹¹ruin is in its midst;
oppression and fraud

---

do not depart from its market-place.
¹²For it is not an enemy who taunts me—
   then I could bear it;
it is not an adversary who deals insolently with me—
   then I could hide from him.
¹³But it is you, a man, my equal,
   my companion, my familiar friend.
¹⁴We used to take sweet counsel together;
   within God's house we walked in the throng.
¹⁵Let death steal over them;
   let them go down to Sheol alive;
   for evil is in their dwelling place and in their heart.
¹⁶But I call to God,
   and the Lord will save me.
¹⁷Evening and morning and at noon
   I utter my complaint and moan,
   and he hears my voice.
¹⁸He redeems my soul in safety
   from the battle that I wage,
   for many are arrayed against me.
¹⁹God will give ear and humble them,
   he who is enthroned from of old,   *Selah*
because they do not change
   and do not fear God.
²⁰My companion stretched out his hand against his friends;
   he violated his covenant.
²¹His speech was smooth as butter,
   yet war was in his heart;
his words were softer than oil,
   yet they were drawn swords.
²²Cast your burden on the Lord,
   and he will sustain you;
he will never permit
   the righteous to be moved.
²³But you, O God, will cast them down
   into the pit of destruction;
men of blood and treachery
   shall not live out half their days.
But I will trust in you.

Psalm 55 was written to help you. According to the title it is a *maskil*. We cannot be certain what that term means, but since it comes from the verb 'to instruct,' the psalm may have been written to share the wisdom of personal experience with fellow strugglers.

Read Psalm 55. Read it again. There is more to it than a cry for help. Read its closing words once more: 'But I will trust in you' (verse 23). Trust, security, peace—that was what the psalmist eventually experienced. That is what we want to experience too. But how can we move from the longing to escape to the security and hope he enjoyed?

A Dark Prospect

David has deep personal problems as we shall see. He is distressed. His living situation simply makes matters worse: 'Destructive forces are at work in the city' (verse 11 NIV). The crime statistics have risen: there is 'violence and strife' (verse 9). But there is also deep decay in personal relationships: 'iniquity and trouble are within it [the city]' (verse 10). On the one hand there is 'oppression' and on the other 'fraud' (verse 11). It is all too common a scene.

The connection between our spiritual and mental well-being and our environment is admittedly complex; but it is obviously a reality. For someone who is going through a time of intense personal struggle, David's environment is not helping any; it simply increases his depression.

Most of us know exactly what David means. In the modern world 'the city' has tended to become synonymous with evil, deprivation, and danger. Sociologists speak about the 'urban flight' as families search for a better, healthier, safer life in the suburbs.

But David is not providing data for sociological analysis. He is speaking about forces let loose in his city that militate against his own spiritual well-being. He cries out to God about the activity of 'the wicked,' an expression that possesses an almost supernatural, demonic connotation in the psalms. Forces beyond human control have been at work. Satan seems to have gained the upper hand.

The name of this city is not mentioned. It could, in theory, be any city. But the psalm's original readers would immediately think about Jerusalem, the city of God. It was there that destructive forces had been released—among the people of God. There was 'violence,' 'strife,' and 'iniquity' within the fellowship of God's people (verses 9-10)!

No wonder David was depressed. Bad enough to experience alienation in the world; far worse to see that the forces of darkness were at work within the city of God, the church, as well.

But there is worse to come. Some of us can cope with obvious enemies. But David has been opposed by someone he had counted among his close friends:

> My companion stretched out his hand
>   against his friends;
> he violated his covenant.
>   His speech was smooth as butter,
> yet war was in his heart;
>   his words were softer than oil,
> yet they were drawn swords.
> (verses 20-21)

He has been betrayed by someone he trusted. He is angry. Of course he is angry!

We do not know the details of his disappointment and pain. He does not tell us. He is writing a *maskil* and he wants his words to be applicable to as many situations as possible.

They may be applicable to a business relationship that has gone wrong. Sadly, the words are all too vivid a description of what happens when churches split. Most obvious of all, they aptly describe the break up of a marriage:

> For it is not an enemy who taunts me—
>   then I could bear it;
> it is not an adversary who deals insolently with me—

> then I could hide from him.
> But it is you, a man, my equal,
>   my companion, my familiar friend.
> We used to take sweet counsel together;
>   within God's house we walked in the throng.
>
> (verses 12-14)

In David's case this is coupled with the hostility of his enemies:

> I am restless in my complaint and I moan,
>   because of the noise of the enemy,
>   because of the oppression of the wicked.
>
> (verses 2-3)

No wonder he cries out,

> My heart is in anguish within me;
>   the terrors of death have fallen upon me.
> Fear and trembling come upon me;
>   and horror overwhelms me.
>
> (verses 4-5)

His whole life has become a catalogue of disappointment and opposition. He feels completely overwhelmed. What is he to do?

> And I say, 'Oh, that I had wings like a dove!
>   I would fly away and be at rest;
> yes, I would wander far away;
>   I would lodge in the wilderness;
> I would hurry to find a shelter,
>   from the raging wind and tempest.'
>
> (verses 6-8)

We have all said it, each in our own way. Our own resources are inadequate for the situation. In any case, the situation is simply too hopeless in and of itself. Flight is our only hope. If only we had the wings of a dove!

That is how most of us respond, even if the flight on 'the wings of a dove' takes a different shape for us today.

What 'wings' do you fly on? What desert place do you make for in order to shelter?

Some of us escape into work, others into leisure; some seek relief in pleasure. Some live in the past—its sorrows as well as its joys and triumphs; others find relief by constant planning for the future. Some escape into lethargy, others into overactivity. The list of 'avoidance' tactics is almost endless. Sadly, many 'escape' into habits and actions that bring permanent ruin to their marriages, homes, families, and even their own bodies. The flight to freedom imprisons them.

But flight can never be a solution. We may thus gain momentary relief, but our situation remains unchanged; indeed, if the truth were told, we become less rather than more able to cope with it.

Furthermore, for the Christian, who knows that God seeks 'truth' or *reality* in the inner person (*Psa.* 51:6), flight can never be a serious option. Yes, we need shelter; but, as we shall see, that is available to us in the city, not in the desert.

What, then, is the right response that David works out in the course of the psalm? It is three-dimensional and involves God, his enemies, and himself.

God

David hardly seems to have realized that from the very beginning of this psalm he has been praying about his situation. Even when he expresses his longing for the 'wings of a dove,' he does so in the presence of God. His words resonate with a sense of God. Here lies the secret of his stability in the face of overwhelming difficulties: he calls upon God 'evening and morning and at noon' (verse 17). For the Jew the new day began at sundown on the previous day, hence the order David uses here.

Perhaps David simply means here to indicate his steadfastness in prayer. It seems likely, however, that, like Daniel (*Dan.* 6:10), he had developed a regular discipline in his life—times of prayer and probably meditation upon God's Word and character; what older Christians would have called a 'quiet time,' or their 'daily devotions.'

Those times were almost certainly his salvation, for two reasons.

1. When we are overwhelmed by our circumstances, our whole life tends to become disordered. This is one of the obvious signs that a person can no longer cope. But we do not always make the connection we should between these basic rhythms in our lives and our personal stability. David kept fixed points in his life. When everything else seemed to collapse, a basic structure was still left, and therefore recovery and rebuilding were still possible.

Remember that, when things overwhelm you and you want to flee. Keep up your basic disciplines and duties. They may seem pointless, like bones without flesh; you may lack the emotional energy to enjoy them or even do them with vigour. You may no longer have a taste for them. But you must not let them collapse. If you do, your defences will be broken down, and rebuilding will become almost impossible.

It is too late to think about this when we feel overwhelmed. We cannot start to build foundations in the middle of a storm; it is too late. Make sure you have begun to build these basic disciplines now. David had obviously done that. He had built strong foundations. When the storm came, of course his instinct was to flee; but, as we shall see, that was not his actual response.

2. There is another reason why this discipline was so important in helping David to weather the storm that broke over him. Serious thought about God steadies us. It elevates our thoughts and our emotions *above* the problems that dominate our lives; it helps us to see that it is not our circumstances but our God and Saviour who is sovereign. We are then able to see our situation in its true light.

As David gives us an example of how he prayed on one of these daily occasions, we see that light slowly begins to dawn, and the noise of the battle begins to subside:

> But I call to God,
>   and the LORD will save me. . .

> he hears my voice.
> He redeems my soul in safety. . .
> *God. . . who is enthroned from of old.*

> (*Psa.* 55:16-19, italics added)

In the middle of disaster he penetrates the dark cloud to see that God reigns and God saves. These are the two most basic doctrines of Scripture. They are also, as David is obviously discovering, the two most practical truths about God we can ever know. No one can meet with God three times each day, seeking his face, studying his Word, without realizing this.

We see the same thing in the life of Daniel, who shared this three-fold devotional discipline. He could easily have authored a lament such as Psalm 55. Surrounded by enemies, betrayed by his colleagues, the desert must have seemed an easier sphere of life than the corridors of power of the Babylonian court. But this was his testimony too:

> Evening and morning and at noon
> I utter my complaint and moan,
> and he hears my voice.
> He redeems my soul in safety.

> (verses 17-18a)

That is exactly the message of Daniel, chapter 6!

But what is particularly impressive about Daniel is that he was conscious from early in his service of God that God reigns over all the circumstances of life and works out his purpose through them. Even when Nebuchadnezzar overwhelmed God's city and people, Daniel realized that it was 'the Lord [who] gave. . . into his hand' (*Dan.* 1:2). 'If our God was sovereign in such dark events, it must have been part of his plan to bring us to Babylon to serve him here,' Daniel reasoned. So he stood against the tide when others around him capitulated; he resolved never to defile himself in Babylon (*Dan.* 1:8). And God redeemed his soul in safety (*Psa.* 55:18).

The same was true of his three companions. Threatened with

the burning furnace for their faithfulness to the God of Israel, they responded with heroic faith. But that heroic faith was rooted in the revelation of God (*Isa.* 43:2):

'If this be so, our God whom we serve is able to deliver us from the burning fiery furnace, and he will deliver us out of your hand, O king. But if not, be it known to you, O king, that we will not serve your gods. . .' (*Dan.* 3:17-18). In either event, they committed themselves to the One they knew who 'in all things. . . works for the good of those who love him, who have been called according to his purpose' (*Rom.* 8:28 NIV).

Sadly, the biblical teaching on the sovereignty of God in his providence has too often been a bone of contention for Christians when it was revealed chiefly as a means of encouragement. It is vital for us to be familiar with it if, like David, Daniel, and his companions, we are to stand in days when our circumstances are liable to overwhelm us.

The Enemies

David's conviction about the sovereignty of God we can understand. But it is clear that a second major element in his response was directed toward the enemies who were a major cause of his sufferings. There is a tone in his voice here that we find more difficult:

> Destroy, O Lord, divide their tongues. . .
> Let death steal over them;
>   let them go down to Sheol alive;
>   for evil is in their dwelling place and in their heart.
>
> (verses 9 and 15)

What are we to make of this? Is depression giving way to anger here?

It has been recognized by counsellors over the centuries that some symptoms of depression disappear with the overt expression of anger. One nineteenth century London physician, a Dr Williams, who was often consulted by patients suffering from mild depression, sometimes referred them to an eminent consultant living in Scotland. Patients who made the journey of several days by coach reached their destination only to discover no such doctor existed. They spent the whole of the return journey planning how they would vent their anger on Dr Williams. They came home furious, but no longer depressed!

Is this what we have in David's case? A chance to 'get it off his chest' by venting his spleen against others?

It may be tempting to read the psalm that way, and to disapprove. Or to point out how far short the Old Testament people fall by comparison with New Testament believers who have been taught by Jesus to love their enemies, just as Paul urges us:

> If your enemy is hungry, feed him;
> if he is thirsty, give him something to drink.
> For by so doing you will heap burning coals on his head.
>
> (*Rom.* 12:20)

The only problem with this interpretation is that both Jesus and Paul are actually expounding the teaching of the Old Testament. In fact Paul is *quoting it!* (see *Prov.* 25:21-22).

Is David, then, sinning?

That would be a 'neat' solution, but it is an inadequate one for several reasons.

1. David's prayer 'Destroy, O Lord, divide their tongues' (verse 9) is an echo of God's own words of judgment on the people who built the tower of Babel: 'Come, let us go down and there *confuse* their language. . . Therefore its name was called Babel, because there the LORD *confused the language* of all the earth' (*Gen.* 11:7, 9, italics added).

David's further wish, 'Let death steal over them . . . for evil is in their dwelling place' (verse 15) must be set in the context of what he goes on to say, 'But you, O God, will cast them down into the pit of destruction. . .' (verse 23).

In both cases he is simply expressing a wish that God would do what God does and will do.

2. In this and other psalms where we find these imprecatory prayers, David is not praying merely as an isolated individual but as the key figure in the kingdom that God is building. He is God's king and ruler. His prayers should not be interpreted as expressions of personal vindictiveness any more than the severe words of a judge against a criminal he is sentencing should be criticized as an outburst of personal animosity.

3. The element of imprecation and terrible judgment is also stubbornly present in the New Testament. We find it on the lips of Jesus and expressed by the pens of all the authors of the New Testament books:

> And will not God give justice to his elect, who cry to him day and night? Will he delay long over them? I tell you, he will give justice to them speedily.
>
> (*Luke* 18:7-8)

> If anyone is preaching to you a gospel contrary to the one you received, let him be accursed.
>
> (*Gal.* 1:9)

> For many, of whom I have often told you and now tell you even with tears, walk as enemies of the cross of Christ. Their end is destruction. . .
>
> (*Phil.* 3:18-19)

> Then he will say to those on his left, 'Depart from me, you cursed, into the eternal fire prepared for the devil and his angels. For I was hungry and you gave me no food. . .' And these will go away into eternal punishment. . .
>
> (*Matt.* 25:41-42, 46)

The Book of Revelation even portrays the *saints in heaven* crying out to God to show his just judgment (*Rev.* 6:10-11). They recognize that there is such a thing as 'the wrath of the Lamb,' in which his enemies are righteously condemned and overthrown (*Rev.* 6:16). In one sense we pray for this daily when we say, 'Your kingdom come. . . your will be done on earth. . .'

There is a righteous instinct at work in David. In some ways it is the beginning of the recovery of equilibrium in his life; he believes that God can do something about his situation. He is manifestly concerned about God's glory and not simply his own difficulties. He has regained his assurance that the wrongs and injustices of life can and will be remedied.

Yet, there is a development within Psalm 55. Earlier in the psalm he is asking for the immediate intervention of divine judgment—'Divide their tongues. . . Let death steal over them' (verses 9, 15). Later, although still in the context of solemn divine judgment, a calmer spirit seems to prevail: 'God will give ear and humble them, he who is enthroned from of old. . . But you, O God, will cast them down. . .' (verses 19, 23).

What is the difference? Earlier in the psalm David was impatient with God, the very God who is so patient with sinners. He had forgotten himself, and he had forgotten his own sinfulness.

Who was David, after all, to complain about betrayal by an intimate friend? Could these words not equally have been written by Uriah the Hittite as he lay dying on the battlefield, the victim of King David's sin?

> For it is not an enemy who taunts me—
>   then I could bear it;
> it is not an adversary who deals
>   insolently with me—
> then I could hide from him.
> But it is you, a man, my equal,
>   my companion, my familiar friend.
> We used to take sweet counsel together;
>   within God's house we walked in the throng.
>
> (verses 12-14)

David had needed a time for mercy; an amnesty from God before the Day of Judgment. The New Testament makes clear that this day of amnesty has been gained by Christ: 'Behold, now is the favourable time, now is the day of salvation'; there is still time to receive the reconciliation (*2 Cor.* 5:20-6:2).

A complex work of grace is now evident in David, but its various strands are clear:

1. In thinking about his enemies he has begun to see that the conflict is not merely a personal vendetta. He belongs to the kingdom of God; a spiritual warfare undergirds these personal experiences. Rather than fly to the desert, he must put on the armour of God and stand in the evil day (*Eph.* 6:10-20).

2. In calling upon God to vindicate his people and destroy his enemies, he began to see how much he himself had needed and had received the mercy of God. Rather than yield to the pressures on his life, and flee to the desert, courage was awakened in him to remain at his post.

The Apostle Paul learned a similar lesson in days of great stress during his ministry in Corinth. But the Lord stood by him and urged him to stay put and serve on. Later he wrote, 'the love of Christ controls us' (*2 Cor.* 5:14)—it left him no choice. He stayed, and many were won to Christ (*Acts* 18:1-11).

3. David learned that the wings of a dove are a poor substitute for trust in the Lord:

> Cast your burden on the LORD,
>   and he will sustain you;
> he will never permit
>   the righteous to be moved.

(verse 22)

'Burden' really means what the Lord has placed upon your shoulders in his providence. 'Roll on to the Lord's shoulders what he has placed on yours' is what he is saying. He has come to see that behind all of his personal circumstances lies the sovereign hand of 'God, who is enthroned from of old' (verse 19). He is able to supply all the help we need to live for him in the circumstances he sets before us.

David does not say, 'and he will take your cares away,' but 'he will sustain you.' The difference is as important as it is obvious. There were still enemies; there was still betrayal; he still lived in the city. The difference was this: David realized that the Lord was still there too.

The same language appears in the story of Elijah. When the brook in the Cherith Ravine dried up during the drought, the Lord said to him: 'Arise, go to Zeraphath, which belongs to Sidon, and dwell there. Behold, I have commanded a widow there *to feed you*' (1 *Kings* 17:9, italics added). The widow woman herself had no lasting resources; but the Lord supplied their needs. 'He will never permit the righteous to be moved' (*Psa.* 55:22).

Can I believe that? When I feel surrounded by enemies of all kinds? When I feel betrayed? When all I want to do is fly away and give up? Yes, I can say, 'But I will trust in you' (verse 23).

Can I really? Can I trust him when he cannot feel what I feel, when he does not understand what it is like?

But he does. He has come to us in Jesus Christ. He understands perfectly. He knows what it is to live in the city.

When he came he was surrounded by enemies.
His soul was overcome with grief and distraction.
He knew what it was for a close companion to betray him.
In Gethsemane he longed that there might be some other way.
But he cast his cares on the Lord. And the Lord sustained him.

When you know that, you can say, 'But I will trust in you' (verse 23).

Slipping Feet

P salms 73 to 83 are a small collection of hymns associated with the name of Asaph. We know little about him apart from the fact that he was a leading singer who became one of the directors of the Jerusalem National Choir (*1 Chron.* 15:17, 19; 16:4-5) and also exercised a prophetic gift (*2 Chron.* 29:30).

What we do know about Asaph stimulates a desire to know him better, not least because he would probably not be the most obvious choice for a contemporary choral director.

We naturally think of upbeat, extrovert, optimistic, energetic Christians as the most likely candidates to lead our church choirs; understandably so! Asaph seems to have been the opposite: downbeat, introspective, melancholic, struggling. Hardly promising material for a music director in a city-centre congregation!

But we would be mistaken if we thought this. For out of this man's heart (interestingly, the most common noun in Psalm 73) came music in the minor key that has given help to multitudes of believers over the centuries. Out of the darkness of the depths he saw the bright glory of the heights of grace. Here, in Psalm 73, we have one of the profoundest of all the psalms.

Asaph begins with what at first sight seems to be a commonplace: 'Truly God is good to Israel' (verse 1). No confession is more fundamental to our faith, or for that matter more obvious than this.

Psalm 73

¹Truly God is good to Israel,
 to those who are pure in heart.
²But as for me, my feet had almost stumbled,
 my steps had nearly slipped.
³For I was envious of the arrogant
 when I saw the prosperity of the wicked.
⁴For they have no pangs until death;
 their bodies are fat and sleek.
⁵They are not in trouble as others are;
 they are not stricken like the rest of mankind.
⁶Therefore pride is their necklace;
 violence covers them as a garment.
⁷Their eyes swell out through fatness;
 their hearts overflow with follies.
⁸They scoff and speak with malice;
 loftily they threaten oppression.
⁹They set their mouths against the heavens,
 and their tongue struts through the earth.
¹⁰Therefore his people turn back to them,
 and find no fault in them.
¹¹And they say, 'How can God know?
 Is there knowledge in the Most High?'
¹²Behold, these are the wicked;
 always at ease, they increase in riches.
¹³All in vain have I kept my heart clean
 and washed my hands in innocence.
¹⁴For all the day long I have been stricken
 and rebuked every morning.
¹⁵If I had said, 'I will speak thus',
 I would have betrayed the generation of your children.
¹⁶But when I thought how to understand this,
 it seemed to me a wearisome task,
¹⁷until I went into the sanctuary of God;
 then I discerned their end.
¹⁸Truly you set them in slippery places;
 you make them fall to ruin.
¹⁹How they are destroyed in a moment,
 swept away utterly by terrors!

> [20]Like a dream when one awakes,
>   O Lord, when you rouse yourself,
> you despise them as phantoms.
> [21]When my soul was embittered,
>   when I was pricked in heart,
> [22]I was brutish and ignorant;
>   I was like a beast towards you.
> [23]Nevertheless, I am continually with you;
>   you hold my right hand.
> [24]You guide me with your counsel,
>   and afterwards you will receive me to glory.
> [25]Whom have I in heaven but you?
>   And there is nothing on earth that I desire besides you.
> [26]My flesh and my heart may fail,
>   but God is the strength of my heart and
> my portion for ever.
> [27]For behold, those who are far from you shall perish;
>   you put an end to everyone who is unfaithful to you.
> [28]But for me it is good to be near God;
>   I have made the Lord GOD my refuge,
>   that I may tell of all your works.

Yet, as with many psalms, the opening words are not merely the introduction to the theme; they spell out the conclusion to which faith has at last come. In Asaph's case, we might add, come as the result of an enormous struggle.

That would have been clearer if verse 1 had been translated 'BUT God is good to Israel.' The introductory expression reappears at significant points in verses 13 and 18. On those occasions a contrast is being drawn. The same is true in verse 1. Asaph is saying: 'Despite everything; in the face of everything in my experience that seems to deny it, I still confess the goodness of God to his people.'

Asaph's confession of the goodness of God is indeed his subject; but his convictions about it were confirmed only slowly and painfully, through a crisis of faith. Indeed, at points, that faith seems almost to subside. He is overwhelmed by the difficulty of believing in the goodness of God in a world like this. He complains that the life of faith is 'in vain' (verse 13); that his 'soul was embittered' (verse 21); that his heart failed (verse 26).

When *Asaph* tells us that God is good, therefore, we know that he really believes it. He is not speaking, ostrich-like, with his head buried in the sand, oblivious to the real world. He has been 'out there' and experienced it. He knows what it is like. He has been through the maze of life's bitter experiences, and now he returns to tell us: 'Yes, but I still can say "God is good to Israel."'

This 'pilgrim's progress' to strengthened faith in the goodness of his God took him through four stages of experience: disaffection; misunderstanding; rediscovery and, finally, satisfaction.

Disaffection

Most of us know what it is like to climb a hill, or a tree, or even to the top of the stairs, and suddenly miss our footing. Only the foot slips, but in that moment the balance of our entire body is threatened. As we regain our balance, we realize how close we were to losing everything.

Asaph felt like that spiritually: 'My feet had almost stumbled; my steps had nearly slipped' (verse 2). One minute he seemed secure; the next there seemed to be no stable ground underneath him.

Eventually he would realize why. He had planted his spiritual feet on theologically unreliable ground.

My family lived at one time on the Island of Unst, the most northerly inhabited island of the Shetland Islands, some 150 miles north of mainland Scotland. Washed by the Gulf Stream as it makes its way northeast, the island was not nearly as cold as one would imagine a place north of the sixtieth parallel (level with Anchorage and St. Petersburg) would be. But it was regularly assaulted by gale-force winds. There cannot be many places in the English-speaking world where church services have been cancelled because of dangerous winds!

Down one side of the island ran steep cliffs, which annually attracted groups of tourists, particularly bird-watchers. Imagine yourself walking along the edge of the cliff; the sea roars, the birds soar, the wind blows. Near the edge of the cliff is the best spot to see nature's magnificence. You marvel at its grandeur. Then, suddenly a gust of wind comes; it unbalances you; your feet slip. You are almost gone!

Thankfully, a strong hand grips you, and you are safe. But you do not easily forget the thoughts that passed through your mind in that split second.

Nor did Asaph. What passed through his mind?

'*I have put my feet in the wrong place.*' He had assumed that if God is good to his people, then, obviously, God's people will be blessed and will prosper. Obedience to God will lead to material plenty, just as disobedience will lead to poverty, so he thought.

There is something remarkably contemporary about this. The message of the 'prosperity gospel' is that God wants to prosper us and make us happy; if we give to him, he will give us our heart's desire: health, wealth, and happiness. Indeed, the whole purpose of the gospel is to enable us to sing 'and now I am happy all the day.' Suffering is no part of it. So we are told.

Elements of the prosperity gospel were alive and well in Asaph's day too; perhaps the majority of his friends unthinkingly believed it. He may have been tempted to believe it himself. But he found it insecure ground, and it soon crumbled under his feet. Something he saw unnerved him.

'*Why do the wicked prosper?*' Asaph was shocked by two things. First of all he realized that contrary to everything he had been led to believe, godless people prospered. Then he was rudely awakened to the fact that he actually envied them!

It is hard to tell which would have been the greater shock. The first was a challenge to muddle-headed theology, but the second shook his spiritual complacency.

What did Asaph see? He saw those who despise God, his Word, and his people doing better than those who love and serve him. They seem to have most of the good fortune; they even seem to suffer less hardship; most of the 'beautiful people' are to be found among them:

> For they have no pangs until death;
> their bodies are fat and sleek.
> They are not in trouble as others are;
> they are not stricken like the rest of mankind.
>
> (verses 4-5)

They go from strength to strength. They exude pride, yet they seem to do better and better materially; they crush those who stand in their way; they seem to be able to swallow heaven and earth; 'always at ease, they increase in riches' (verse 12).

Meanwhile the godly have their backs against the wall:

> For all the day long I have been stricken
> and rebuked every morning.
>
> (verse 14)

It all seems wrong, desperately wrong. Not only is Asaph searching for an answer to the question '*Why do bad things happen to good people?*', he is also troubled by another question: '*Why do so many good things happen to bad people?*'

Those who publicly flaunt their immorality can earn endless millions in the process, and their people turn back to them, and find no fault in them. 'And they say, "How can God know? Is there knowledge in the Most High?"' (verses 10-11). Where is the goodness of God in a world like this?

I wonder what age Asaph was. Apparently up until now the prosperity of the wicked had passed him by; now he was beginning to notice it. He was beginning to ask whether the life of faith was really worth it; did it even make sense?

There comes a time in the lives of many men and women committed to Christ when similar questions arise.

You may be one of them. You have been living for Christ, serving him, obeying his Word. These have been the most important things in life to you. Since your teenage years or student days, perhaps, doing his will has been the dominant drive in your life, no matter what the sacrifice involved.

In fact, you have never really thought of serving Christ as involving sacrifices. You never gave much thought to material possessions; you knew that you had a far greater treasure in Christ. What he wanted was more important than position, or salary, homes, and possessions. So you went into some form of Christian service, became a pastor, or a teacher in a Christian school, or went overseas as a missionary. Or, perhaps you sacrificed your career because you wanted to devote yourself to being a mother, bringing up a family, giving yourself to them without reserve.

But for some reason you have recently begun to notice your contemporaries! They were no more intelligent than you at school; no nicer than you in personality, certainly! But look at them! See the cars they drive; the house they own (now mortgage free!); the schools their children attend; the clubs to which they belong; the vacations they can take. And they would not give a penny for your Christ! They are slightly embarrassed, perhaps even a little surprised that you have not done as well as they have. But then they remember you became 'religious'!

I still wince slightly when I remember a friend telling me that my name had somehow cropped up in a conversation with one of his clients who had known me when we were both teenagers. The client asked what I was doing with my life, and when he heard the answer, expressed great astonishment: 'My! I'm surprised; I thought he would have done well in life!'

Where has your Christian devotion led you? As I write, I could compose a lengthy list of well-educated, highly gifted contemporaries who have devoted themselves to serving the Lord whose ill health or the burden of living within their small financial means might tempt them to say:

> For I was envious of the arrogant
>   when I saw the prosperity of the wicked. . .
> All in vain have I kept my heart clean
>   and washed my hands in innocence.
> For all the day long I have been stricken. . .
>
>   (verses 3, 13-14)

Where is God's goodness to his people in this?

In his moment of doubt, Asaph was in a dangerous position. He felt he was losing his safe foothold. But he was at least being real. He would later discover that what he saw was not the whole truth, and therefore not the real truth. But for the moment it was real enough to him, and in expressing it honestly he was taking the first step to resolve the problem.

That is an example we should follow. 'Spit it out' we used to say when we could see that something was on a friend's mind. It is wise spiritual counsel. As in Asaph's case, it helps us to see where our thinking has begun to go wrong.

Misunderstanding

Asaph tried desperately to make sense of his world, but he admits, 'When I thought how to understand this, it seemed to me a wearisome task' (verse 16). Now as he seeks to discover the hand of God, he realizes that he has been guilty of a serious misunderstanding— not so much of human nature, but of God's wisdom and ways.

He had forgotten that he was a creature. He had tried to interpret his experiences in his own wisdom. The effort simply gave him a headache.

Later he tells us he ended up with an embittered soul and a pricked heart (verse 21). Now he saw what he had done in its true light:

he had behaved like a beast (verse 22), 'brutish and ignorant.' He thought he could solve his problem by answering his question, 'Why are these things happening?' He learned that his problem could only be resolved by remembering who he was: a creature, with limited understanding, yet one who belonged to a God of infinite understanding who could be trusted to fulfil his own perfect purposes.

Job discovered the same thing in a somewhat more dramatic way. He too had engaged in trying to understand why it is that the righteous suffer, only to feel that he was beating his head against a wall.

> Then the LORD answered Job out of the whirlwind and said:
> 'Who is this that darkens counsel by words
> without knowledge?
> Dress for action like a man; I will question you,
> and you make it known to me.'
>
> *(Job* 38:1-3)

Job, like Asaph, has been questioning God; yes, questioning God! As though a child were in a position to understand all that his father had planned.

The Lord then sets before Job a magnificent vision of the wonders of his creation. It is a theatre in which he displays the brilliance of his wisdom. This humbles Job's pride.

> Then Job answered the LORD and said:
> "I know that you can do all things, and that no purpose of
> yours can be thwarted.
> 'Who is this that hides counsel without knowledge?'
> Therefore I have uttered what I did not understand,
> things too wonderful for me, which I did not know.
> 'Hear, and I will speak;
> I will question you, and you make it known to me.'
> I had heard of you by the hearing of the ear,
> but now my eye sees you;
> therefore I despise myself,
> and repent in dust and ashes"
>
> *(Job* 42:1-6)

Like Job, Asaph had forgotten his identity. He had lost sight of the fact that he was a child of God. God's ways with his children are not those his children would choose in their own unaided wisdom. But, then, God's purposes and goals are different from those pursued by the world. He is more concerned with the character of his children than their wealth; he is committed to their Christ-likeness rather than their indulgence; he desires their progress in obedience rather than their material prosperity.

At last it dawned on Asaph and he realized that his first line of reasoning was a denial of all that it meant to belong to the family of God:

> If I had said, 'I will speak thus,'
> I would have betrayed the generation of your children
>
> (verse 15)

The Book of Proverbs would teach this in words that the author of Hebrews later found illumined the whole of life:

> And have you forgotten the exhortation [in *Prov.* 3:11-12]
> that addresses [*notice the present tense*] you *as sons*:
> 'My son, do not regard lightly the discipline of the Lord,
> nor be weary when reproved by him.
> For the Lord disciplines the one he loves,
> and he chastises every son whom he receives.'
>
> (*Heb.* 12:5-6, italics added)

Not to share in such discipline is not to be a true child of God (*Heb.* 12:8)! Yes, such child-training is painful, but it is fruitful and creates true godliness and righteousness.

This sheds a different light on Asaph's words in verse 14:

> For all day long have I been stricken
> and rebuked every morning

Perhaps, like ourselves, there is something of childish fretfulness in this ('You *never* let me do it' says the child who has been refused it for the first time!).

The point is clear. The experience of the people of God is unattractive to the worldly eye, which looks for and is impressed only by present gain and material profit. But neither of these lasts, nor do they produce the likeness to Christ that makes things permanent.

Listen to Paul:

> The Spirit himself bears witness with our spirit that we are children of God, and if children, then heirs—heirs of God and fellow heirs with Christ, provided we suffer with him in order that we may also be glorified with him. For I consider that the sufferings of this present time are not worth comparing with the glory that is to be revealed to us.
>
> (*Rom.* 8:16-18)

> For this slight momentary affliction is preparing for us an eternal weight of glory beyond all comparison. . .
>
> (*2 Cor.* 4: 17)

Listen to Jesus:

> Do not lay up for yourselves treasures on earth, where moth and rust destroy and where thieves break in and steal, but lay up for yourselves treasures in heaven, where neither moth nor rust destroys and where thieves do not break in and steal. For where your treasure is, there your heart will be also.
>
> (*Matt.* 6:19-21)

Asaph was beginning to hear a faint echo of that in God's dealings with him. Soon something else would make it even clearer to him.

Rediscovery

'But when I thought how to understand this, it seemed to me a wearisome task,' said Asaph, 'until I went into the sanctuary of God' (verses 16-17).

What was this sanctuary experience? Everyone who studies this psalm seriously asks that question; it is not surprising that a wide variety of answers has been suggested.

Perhaps something dramatic happened while he was in the temple precincts. Did he, quite literally, see the 'final destiny' of the wicked? Did one of them die suddenly of a heart attack while hypocritically participating in a worship service? Of all places for the ungodly to die—in the presence of the living God into whose hands it is a fearful thing to fall!

Or, did Asaph have an experience like Isaiah's? Did he have a new sense of the Lord being exalted and enthroned on the praises of his people (*Psa.* 22:3)? We do not know. What seems certain, however, is this: in the presence of God, among his worshiping people, he saw life in a different perspective altogether. More exactly, he now saw things as they seem in the light of eternity—including the truth about those whose lifestyles he had earlier envied. In a moment of divine illumination he 'discerned their end.'

He gives us two pictures of it:

1. They are standing 'in slippery places' (verse 18). He felt himself to be in danger of slipping. Now, in the presence of God he saw that the ground on which the ungodly stand is actually sinking sand.

Until we look at the foundations, sin seems secure; but in fact those who sin have no stable ground under their feet. At any moment all that they have built may collapse and be gone. Then they will have nothing.

But Asaph, whose foothold had almost slipped, had solid foundations on which to build his life: the character and promise of God, the worship of his house, the fellowship of his people, a secure destiny:

> On the Rock of Ages founded,
> > What can shake thy sure repose?
> With salvation's walls surrounded,
> > Thou may'st smile at all thy foes.

By contrast, 'How they are destroyed in a moment, swept away utterly by terrors' (verse 19).

2. The prosperous wicked seem so real, as does their prosperity; but in the sight of God they are insubstantial and ephemeral: 'Like a dream when one awakes, O Lord, when you rouse yourself, you despise them as phantoms.' (verse 20).

> Let the world deride or pity,
>   I will glory in thy Name.
> Fading is the worldling's pleasure,
>   All his boasted pomp and show;
> Solid joys and lasting treasure
>   None but Zion's children know.
>
> *John Newton*

Asaph had viewed life through the wrong end of the telescope. No wonder man had seemed great and significant while God seemed small and obscure! No wonder spiritual realities seemed light while material things seemed weighty. But then he entered the sanctuary of God! In God he found there was sanctuary, protection, and deliverance from his false perceptions. In God's light he saw light (*Psa.* 36:9).

We must not lose sight of the simplest and most obvious lesson that Asaph teaches us here. Remember what he became—the choir director, the leader of the praises of God's people. He was qualified to be so because the temple meant so much to him. There he met with God.

That, ultimately, is the effect on us of true worship. When God is enthroned on the praises of his people, when in prayer we have access to his throne, when the exposition of Scripture raises the affections of God's people as high as possible, as Jonathan Edwards used to say it should do, then we know a little of what it means to sing that 'heaven came down and glory filled my soul'; we are 'lost in wonder, love and praise.' God seems glorious and man small.

The worship of God provides the true scales on which to weigh up the experiences of life. In his presence alone can we answer the questions: What is this really worth? Where will it really end?

That is why the author of Hebrews wrote to discouraged Christians whose feet were almost slipping: 'And let us consider how to stir up one another. . . not neglecting to meet together. . .' (*Heb.* 10:24-25). Such neglect prevents us from sharing Asaph's experience.

Asaph's vision of ungodly man's final destiny is deeply solemnizing. It is reminiscent of the words of the first psalm:

> The wicked are not so,
> but are like chaff that the wind drives away.
>
> (*Psa.* 1:4)

Even the language in which they are described—short, staccato statements—contrasts with the longer flowing statements that describe the destiny of the righteous:

> He is like a tree planted by streams of water
> that yields its fruit in its season
> and its leaf does not wither.
>
> (*Psa.* 1:3)

Yes, 'Solid joys. . . None but Zion's children know.'

Satisfaction

The destiny of the wicked has been made clear to Asaph in the presence of God; so too is the future of the believer, both now and hereafter. God will rectify all wrongs. His psalm closes with a beautiful expression of contented faith. He is no longer gazing on himself and relying on his own resources to interpret his experiences; he is gazing upon the character and ways of God in the beauty of his holiness.

Thus Asaph expounds the ways of God to men. He gives us a biblical version of what we technically call a 'theodicy,' a justification of the biblical view of God and his ways. There are some things worth learning from its pattern even though he is not writing a piece of apologetic theology.

1. Asaph gives us a limited theodicy. He recognizes that life is full of mystery. While he believes that God understands all things, Asaph

knows he does not. But he sees that God has given sufficient evidence of both his love and his righteousness in a sinful world. That is enough to persuade him that it is reasonable to trust in the Lord even though he cannot understand all his ways. Since God is infinite in his understanding, power, and wisdom, that is hardly surprising!

2. Those who reject the biblical view of God generally begin with the assumption that man is morally good, or morally neutral. He deserves to experience good things. Asaph begins with the presupposition that man is now a sinner, and that he has no inherent right that one single good thing should happen to him. That puts a different complexion on the problem of our suffering.

3. Opponents of the biblical teaching on God insist that Christians should answer all their questions now. Asaph believes that many questions, and indeed some part of every question, will be answered only in the hereafter.

4. Opponents of the biblical teaching on God will trust him only if their reason can first understand him. Asaph saw that in the very nature of the case (God is infinite, we are finite; he is holy, we are sinful) we must learn first to trust him in the light of his revelation. Then we will grow in our ability to understand him.

Asaph's heart may fail; but the Lord is everything to him. He is always beside him and holds on to him when he is in danger of falling (verse 23). He guides him with the counsel of his Word now; later he will bring him to his glory. And so he sings out:

> Whom have I in heaven but you?
> And there is nothing on earth that I desire besides you.
>
> (verse 25)

He had coveted the circumstances of the ungodly; now he sees how unreliable and temporary those circumstances are. All he wants in heaven and on earth is to know that God is his and he is God's.

Asaph had begun to question the goodness of God because of the nature of the world in which he lived. Now his perspective is completely different. He realizes that by faith he lives in the very presence of the good God—'it is good to be near God' (verse 28).

He no longer makes the mistake of thinking that everything is inherently good in itself. Things do not naturally all 'work out for the good.' The reverse is the case. Life in a fallen world is good only because we can never be separated from the good God (*Rom.* 8:39) who 'works for the good of those who love him, who have been called according to his purpose' (*Rom.* 8:28 NIV).

With open eyes Asaph saw 'tribulation. . . distress. . . persecution. . . famine. . . nakedness. . . danger. . . sword' (*Rom.* 8:35). 'Yes,' he replies, 'but God is good to Israel.' If this God is for us, who can be against us?

Can you say that too?

. . . .

8

Singing the Blues

We should read the psalms out loud to feel their full weight and power; none more so than Psalm 102. It makes for harrowing reading.

There is a long-standing tradition, from the days of the early church, of interpreting this psalm as one of the seven penitential psalms (*Psalms* 6, 32, 38, 51, 102, 130, 143). It was believed to contain the classical elements of true repentance: conviction of sin, sorrow for it, repentance from it, and forgiveness.

It is clear that this is a mistake. Psalm 102 does not describe a sinful man experiencing repentance, but a deeply depressed saint finding deliverance. He does so not by confessing his sin (there is no word of sorrow for sin in the entire psalm) but by complaining to God.

Indeed one of the healing elements in the psalm lies in the fact that it is an explosion of emotion. The psalmist has come to an end of his ability to keep his feelings tightly controlled; the cork is off, and he pours out the poison in his soul that has been gathering over many days.

This, then, is a lament, a soul-journey downward before it becomes an ascent of the spirit. Yet this depressed individual is obviously a choice believer, a faithful servant of God. He is one of the inspired penmen of Scripture! Indeed, he was a prophet. Nevertheless, he is deeply distressed and depressed. He is struggling simply to keep his head above water. The title perfectly describes him: he is afflicted and faint, and he pours out his lament before the Lord.

Psalm 102

[1]Hear my prayer, O LORD;
  let my cry come to you!
[2]Do not hide your face from me
  in the day of my distress!
Incline your ear to me;
  answer me speedily in the day when I call!
[3]For my days pass away like smoke,
  and my bones burn like a furnace.
[4]My heart is struck down like grass and has withered;
  I forget to eat my bread.
[5]Because of my loud groaning
  my bones cling to my flesh.
[6]I am like a desert owl of the wilderness,
  like an owl of the waste places;
[7]I lie awake;
  I am like a lonely sparrow on the housetop.
[8]All the day my enemies taunt me;
  those who deride me use my name for a curse.
[9]For I eat ashes like bread
  and mingle tears with my drink,
[10]because of your indignation and anger;
  for you have taken me up and thrown me down.
[11]My days are like an evening shadow;
  I wither away like grass.
[12]But you, O LORD, are enthroned for ever;
  you are remembered throughout all generations.
[13]You will arise and have pity on Zion;
  it is the time to favour her;
  the appointed time has come.
[14]For your servants hold her stones dear
  and have pity on her dust.
[15]Nations will fear the name of the LORD,
  and all the kings of the earth will fear your glory.
[16]For the LORD builds up Zion;
  he appears in his glory;
[17]he regards the prayer of the destitute
  and does not despise their prayer.
[18]Let this be recorded for a generation to come,

> so that a people yet to be created may praise the Lord:
> [19]that he looked down from his holy height;
> from heaven the LORD looked at the earth,
> [20]to hear the groans of the prisoners,
> to set free those who were doomed to die,
> [21]that they may declare in Zion the name of the LORD,
> and in Jerusalem his praise,
> [22]when peoples gather together,
> and kingdoms, to worship the LORD.
> [23]He has broken my strength in midcourse;
> he has shortened my days.
> [24]'O my God,' I say, 'take me not away
> in the midst of my days—
> you whose years endure
> throughout all generations!'
> [25]Of old you laid the foundation of the earth,
> and the heavens are the work of your hands.
> [26]They will perish, but you will remain;
> they will all wear out like a garment.
> You will change them like a robe, and they will pass away,
> [27]but you are the same, and your years have no end.
> [28]The children of your servants shall dwell secure;
> their offspring shall be established before you.

We instinctively feel that this ought not to be. Christians should not get depressed. There are certainly teachers and preachers who will reinforce that instinct. But we have already seen that the New Testament tells us that Jesus was depressed when the occasion warranted it, as it did on the eve of his death. There is no sin, or even necessarily failure, in feeling depressed; the important question is: How do we respond to it and handle it? It is here that Psalm 102 offers us its painful but wise analysis.

We have a saying that 'misery seeks company.' But depression has a tendency to isolate us. We feel we are alone and that our experience is unique. This psalm immediately tells the depressed: you are not alone! Someone has been there before you. Through this psalm he has come to guide you through the darkness into the light.

One of the most important features about Psalm 102 is that it has a turning point, in verses 11 and 12:

> My days are like an evening shadow;
>   I wither away like grass.
> But you, O LORD. . .

The question is: how did he get to that turning point and where did it eventually lead him? *And how can we?* Let us follow him on his pilgrimage through depression.

Interior Pilgrimage

Life is dark for the afflicted man, and the darkness is very deep. It surrounds him while God seems distant, hidden from him in an impenetrable cloud. The heavens seem like brass as he prays. God does not seem to hear him. His prayers feel like arrows that fall short of their target. He is simply too far away for God to hear him, although he cries out from the depth of his need:

> *Hear* my prayer, O LORD;
> *let* my cry come to you.
>   (verse 1, italics added)

His great fear is that, in his hour of deepest need, the Lord is hiding his face from him.

The hiding of the face of God was a cause of repeated anxiety among the psalmists and prophets in the Old Testament. God had given the Aaronic blessing to his people, promising that his face would be turned toward them and would shine upon them. He would be gracious to them (*Num.* 6:22-27). In this way God named them as his own possession and responsibility.

The pronouncing of these words meant as much to the Old Testament believer as singing words such as George Wade Robinson's do to Christians:

His for ever, only His;
　　Who the Lord and me shall part?
Ah, with what a rest of bliss
　　Christ can fill the loving heart!
Heaven and earth may fade and flee,
　　First-born light in gloom decline,
But while God and I shall be, I am his and he is mine.

But what do you do when they no longer seem true? When your cry for help does not seem to you to reach God; when his face seems hidden; when his ear seems deliberately turned away so that he cannot hear you—where does that leave you?

When we have a physical problem and 'complain' to our physician about it, he may do various tests and send 'samples' (of our blood, for example) for analysis. The analysis of these samples will provide clues to exactly what the problem is.

We can profitably imitate that procedure when it comes to spiritual difficulties too. In the preface to his exposition of the Psalms, the reformer John Calvin insightfully refers to them as 'an anatomy of all the parts of the soul.' What, then, do we find in the 'blood sample' that the author of Psalm 102 provides for us?

Three elements have come together to affect his spirits and create his deep sense of depression.

Physical

He is a sick man. He describes his symptoms graphically: 'my bones burn like a furnace. . . my bones cling to my flesh' (verses 3, 5). He is a gaunt and emaciated figure, devoid of strength. He seems, in fact, to be near to death.

We do not all experience depression in this way when we are sick, even seriously sick. But we all need to recognize that there is a connection between the condition of our bodies and that of our 'spirits.'

We sometimes use that old-fashioned language when we ask friends what 'kind of spirits' they are in. We mean: are you cheerful, optimistic, enthusiastic, or are you downcast, pessimistic, struggling? We are rarely surprised if someone says, 'I'm feeling a bit low today, I have the "flu".' We know from experience that bodily ailments affect us in that way.

Scripture explains the reason for this: God has made us as a physical and spiritual unity; we are not two separate entities, body and spirit, existing in isolation from each other. We are men and women living in two spheres, physical and spiritual; what happens to us in the one affects us in the other.

We should expect to find our spirits depressed when we are unwell! The important thing is how we respond. For some the battle may be fiercer than for others. But we should not make the mistake of thinking that the difficulty of the battle is an indication of our spiritual poverty, or a sign that we are not Christians at all.

Most Christians know the name of the great Victorian preacher Charles Haddon Spurgeon. The schedule of his ministry is breathtaking by any standard (several sermons each week, always new; an enormous list of publications; a congregation of thousands; an orphanage and pastor's college to support; a vast correspondence; an astounding amount of reading). But neither achievements such as these, nor spirituality such as his, safeguard us from experiencing deep melancholy when we are ill (as he frequently was). Read beyond the eloquence of the language of this letter to his congregation to feel the pain:

> Dear Friends,
>
> The Furnace still glows around me. Since I last preached to you, I have been brought very low; my flesh has been tortured with pain, *and my spirit has been prostrate with depression. . .*
>
> I am as a potter's vessel when it is utterly broken, useless and laid aside. Nights of watching and days of weeping have been mine.[1]

[1] C. H. Spurgeon, *The Full Harvest*, (Edinburgh: Banner of Truth Trust, 1973), p. 195. [Italics added].

Physical exhaustion, not least in spiritual service and conflict, can have the same effect on us—as Elijah discovered.

God prescribed rest for his weary and depressed prophet (*1 Kings* 19:1-9). More powerful medical remedies may be necessary in other circumstances. We are frail, complex human structures with bodies liable to weakness and disease. Knowing that our physical condition can affect our spirits helps us to understand ourselves, our moods, our times of melancholy.

It also leads us to ask how God enables us to respond. But we must first notice that there were other infectious elements in what the psalmist 'poured out' from his soul.

Chronological

His melancholy also had a 'chronological' character to it in the sense that it came over him in waves; sometimes during the day, sometimes during the night.

Day by Day. Concerning his waking hours he says:

> For my days pass away like smoke. . .
> I forget to eat my bread. . .
> All the day my enemies taunt me; . . .
> I. . . mingle tears with my drink, . . .
> My days are like an evening shadow.
>
> (verses 3, 4, 8, 9, 11)

We do not need a trained psychiatrist to explain these symptoms to us. Every 'home doctor' book will tell us that these are classic symptoms of depression. Consider them:

One day becomes very much like another; nothing important happens, nothing to lift or change the spirits.

Our appetite has gone. We allow ourselves to get into a vicious circle. We need to eat to live, but we have little taste for either food or life. We forget what an important role food and meals have in our lives. Meals are social occasions; but we cannot face company.

Meal times are regulators, subtle disciplinarians of the way we use time.

This is surely something worth noting. Great musicians, singers, and even sportsmen recognize how important the basic disciplines are—scales, stance, grip, rhythm. If those fundamental disciplines are not in place, everything becomes disordered.

No doubt this psalmist had good reason to feel in low spirits. But he had made a cardinal error in allowing his depression to control the structure of his daily existence. When it dominates everything, almost nothing can shift it.

Depression took the place of food; tears came even at the effort to take a drink. Whatever he did, his melancholy haunted him, so that one day was the same as another, one activity as meaningless as another. All routine had gone. Meaning and structure in his life had crumbled.

An additional facet appears in verse 8: 'All the day my enemies taunt me. . .' Perhaps that was literally the case. But other things he says suggest that he had actually isolated himself from other people. He met neither friends nor enemies.

He seems, in fact, to have developed something of a persecution complex. No doubt the opposition to him, for whatever reason, was real enough. But was it as incessant and persistent as he suggests? He speaks as someone who not only experiences depression but has become a prisoner to it. He had lost his sense of proportion.

Night by Night. In the night the seed of depression is fertilized and becomes a plant; if it is a dwarf that pursues us during the day, it becomes a giant that overpowers us during the night:

> I am like a desert owl of the wilderness,
>> like an owl of the waste places;
> I lie awake;
>> I am like a lonely sparrow on the housetop.

> (verses 6-7)

Depressed during the day, he tastes desolating isolation at night. He cannot sleep; he cannot control his mind; he cannot think positive thoughts. The description is a chilling, but only too real one, reminiscent of the owl in Thomas Gray's famous *Elegy Written in a Country Churchyard*:

> Save that from yonder ivy-mantled tow'r
> > The moping owl does to the moon complain
> Of such as, wand'ring near her secret bow'r
> > Molest her ancient solitary reign.

In his travelogue *The Land and the Book*, W. Thomson describes his first sighting of this 'desert owl':

> It was certainly the most sombre, austere bird I ever saw. *It gave one the blues simply to look at it.* David could find no more expressive type of solitude and melancholy by which to illustrate his own sad state.[2]

He is a brother in sorrow with Asaph, the choir director, who perfectly describes his state of mind:

> . . . in the night my hand is stretched out
> > without wearying;
> > *my soul refuses to be comforted.*
>
> (*Psa.* 77:2, italics added)

The verb *refused* is used earlier in Scripture of Jacob, when his sons brought back Joseph's robe covered in blood. He drew the logical (if erroneous) conclusion that his son had been torn to death by a wild animal. 'All his sons and all his daughters rose up to comfort him, but he *refused to be comforted*. . .' (*Gen.* 37:35, italics added). An even more familiar use is found in Jeremiah 31:15: '. . .Rachel is weeping for her children; she refuses to be comforted for her children, because they are no more.' This is the refusal of comfort that arises from being in the grip of despair.

---

[2] W. H. Thomson, *The Land and the Book*, new edition edited by J. Grande (London: 1910), p. 240. [Italics added].

It is important to notice this element of deliberate choice, especially since we have underlined that the psalmist does have objective reasons for his melancholy. Those reasons are involuntary; but to refuse comfort is an act of the will for which he bears personal responsibility; he could have done otherwise.

Do you see the point? Having reasons for his feelings of depression was not an adequate reason for being mastered by them. His depression was not inevitable.

Even if a complete cure was not immediately available (so long as he is sick, this man may be prone to these spirits), a measure of relief was. But he has come to the stage where he refuses to take the medicine that is available to him.

To say this to him might seem at first sight to be devastatingly cruel. But there is a time to be cruel in order to be kind. Jesus, remember, once asked a chronically sick man if he wanted to get better (*John* 5:6). Yes, deep sympathy was needed; his situation was horrific in every respect. But the surgeon does not ordinarily regard the patient's illness as a reason not to use his scalpel. Rather the reverse. Only the scalpel's cut will save and heal. That was the case here. We should note it well.

Satanic

There is, in addition to these first two elements, something about the psalmist's experience that can only be described as satanic. Not in the sense that he was demon-possessed. There is no evidence of that whatsoever. But consider his address to the Lord:

> You have taken me up and thrown me down.
>
> (verse 10)

Can that be true? Does God take his people up and play with them, like a giant destructive wave tossing swimmers high in its surging power, only to thrust them cruelly into the depths to destroy them? Is Shakespeare's King Lear right?

As flies to wanton boys, are we to the gods,
They kill us for their sport.[3]

Everything in us should cry out, 'No!' The psalmist could not be more seriously wrong. In his physical, spiritual, and mental frailty he has succumbed to a sinister satanic temptation.

'It is Satan's practice to go over the hedge where it is lowest,' writes Richard Sibbes, a master soul-comforter of an earlier century.[4] He could have been describing the experience of our psalmist. In fact much that Sibbes writes about the subtle working of Satan rings true to Psalm 102:

> The soul is often cast down by Satan, who is all for casting down and disquieting. . . when he [Satan] seeth men will to heaven, and that they have good title to it, then he follows them with all dejecting and uncomfortable temptations that he can. It is his continual trade and course to seek his rest in our disquiet, he is by beaten practice and profession a tempter of this kind.[5]

> There is cause oft in the body of those in whom a melancholy temper prevaileth. Darkness makes men fearful. Melancholy persons are in a perpetual darkness, all things seem black and dark unto them. . . the sweetest comforts are not lightsome enough unto those that are deep in melancholy. . . whatever is presented to a melancholy person, comes in a dark way to the soul. . . how fit are they then to judge of things removed from sense, as of their spiritual estate in Christ?[6]

> How many imagine their failings to be fallings, and their fallings to be fallings away. . . unto which misapprehensions, weak and dark spirits are subject. And Satan, as a cunning rhetorician, here enlargeth the fancy, to apprehend things bigger than they are?[7]

---

[3] William Shakespeare, *King Lear*, 4.1.38.
[4] R. Sibbes, 'The Soul's Conflict', in *Works of Richard Sibbes*, 7 vols (Reprint, Edinburgh: Banner of Truth Trust, 2001), 1.142.
[5] Ibid., p. 134.
[6] Ibid., p. 136.
[7] Ibid., p. 137.

But is this a true analysis of what has happened in this man's life? Admittedly there is no mention of Satan anywhere in the psalm itself. But the conclusion the writer has drawn about the character of God is precisely the view of God with which Satan tempted Adam and Eve in the Garden of Eden: 'God has set you in this magnificent garden with its delicious and beautiful fruits,' he said. 'He has lifted you up; but didn't he say that you were not to eat from any of these trees?' (*Gen.* 3:1).

What was Satan doing? Formally he was tempting Adam and Eve to doubt the authority of God's Word. But in an even more sinister way he was distorting their understanding of God's character. He insinuated that God treated them like playthings, maliciously and spitefully setting wonderful blessings before them, but denying them the enjoyment of them all.

The psalmist had succumbed to a similar temptation. God, who had given so many covenant promises that he would bless his people, had proved to be no more than a cynical potentate, discarding them for his own amusement. This was his bitter conclusion.

This is a hidden secret in many Christians' lives. A voice is heard in the depths of the soul saying that God cannot *really* be trusted; he is not *really* gracious. This psalmist, despite being rich in spiritual experience, heard it clearly when he had no resources to resist it. It was the voice of the serpent; and it almost broke him. It certainly brought him to the lowest point in the entire psalm.

'Satan's aim is to drive the saint to madness by despair,' writes Calvin.[8] He sometimes does so by leading us to attribute to God characteristics that actually belong to Satan.

Remember Job? We know from the prologue to his story that he was attacked and assaulted by Satan (*Job* 1-2). But everyone who gave him counsel urged him to see his suffering as a direct punishment from God for his sin. He was thus brought to the verge of blaming

---

[8] John Calvin, *Institutes of the Christian Religion*, 1.18.1.

God for what Satan was doing. The consequences would have been disastrous if God had not stepped in.

At one point Job came to the verge of despair:

> If I summoned him and he answered me,
>> I would not believe that he was listening to my voice.
> For he crushes me with a tempest
>> and multiplies my wounds without cause;
> he will not let me get my breath,
>> but fills me with bitterness. . .
> I am blameless; I regard not myself;
>> I loathe my life.
> It is all one; therefore I say,
>> He destroys both the blameless and the wicked. . .
>> *if it is not he, who then is it?*
>
> (*Job* 9:16-18,21-22,24, italics added)

If we were spectators of the drama of Job's sufferings in a theatre, we would have to restrain ourselves from shouting out to him: 'Job, it isn't God. God loves you! Job, don't you see that this is the hand of Satan? Job! It's Satan, not God!' The same is true when we hear the psalmist say of God, 'You have taken me up and thrown me down.'

Yet these last words, which bring him to his lowest point, also prove to be the turning point in the whole experience. He has come to an end of himself. His own resources are finished. For all his fears, he still knows that his only hope lies in God. As Luther well put it: 'When God seems to be my enemy, and to stand with a drawn sword against me, then I cast myself and throw myself into his arms.'

The Soul's Ascent

What turned the psalmist round? The opening words of the second half of the psalm give us one clue: 'But you, O LORD' (verse 12). The title of the psalm gives us another: 'A prayer. . . pours out his complaint before the LORD.'

This should not be misunderstood as though someone had said to him, 'Prayer will make everything all right.' It was not because of any power inherent in prayer that he was given a measure of ability to overcome his depression; it was because prayer involves no longer focusing or depending on ourselves and our own resources. It means turning to God and his resources.

Before, he had been turned inside on himself; now he was turned to the Lord. An index of this is that in verses 1 to 11 there are twenty-six occurrences of 'I,' 'me,' and 'my'; in verses 12 to 28, apart from verses 23 and 24, there are none!

The poison had been bottled up in him; now he opened his soul to God and poured it out before him. Now he began to talk! The effect was dramatic. As he poured out the poison from his soul, his spirit was vivified, the effect of the spiritual poison was alleviated.

'Spit it out' we say to a child who has swallowed some harmful liquid. That is what our Father says to us when he sees us in this psalmist's melancholy spirit. 'Come on now,' he says to us, 'spit it out.' He listens, patiently; he hears; he comes near; he assures us of his love. We begin to recover.

In prayer he also began to talk *to God*. In Psalms 42 and 43 we saw the importance of talking to our souls, not simply listening to them. Here we learn another lesson in spiritual rhetoric: to talk *about God* rather than *about ourselves*.

Here too the psalmist's progressive deliverance is indexed in the language he uses. In verses 1 to 11 the great covenant name of God, the Lord (*Yahweh*) is used only once (in verse 1); in verses 12 to 22 it is used seven times (verses 12, 15, 16, 18, 19, 21, 22).

Notice, however, that in verses 23 and 24, he appears to begin to slip back again into pain and melancholy:

> He has broken my strength in midcourse;
> he has shortened my days.
> 'O my God,' I say, 'take me not away in the
> midst of my days. . .'

But even here he does not slide back into the morass of hopelessness in which we earlier found him. He wants to live! He wants to be comforted! His spiritual recovery may not follow a straight-line graph; he slips back again. But he does not slip so far this time. How could he, now that he has the Lord in his vision?

In these words lies the reason for his deliverance from terrible depression: he has the Lord in his vision, in every direction.

He looks *upward* to the sovereign power of God in heaven and on earth:

> But you, O LORD, are enthroned forever. . .
>> Nations will fear the name of the LORD,
> and all the kings of the earth will fear your glory.
>
> (verses 12, 15)

The God who rules over nature and the nations is able to rule over his own troubled heart and exercise his sovereign power over his troubled circumstances too.

He looks *backward* to the unchanging mercy of God in words that describe God's compassion toward his broken (and doubtless deeply depressed) people at the time of the Exodus (cf. *Exod.* 2:23-25):

> . . . He looked down from his holy height;
>> from heaven the LORD looked at the earth,
> to hear the groans of the prisoners,
>> to set free those who were doomed to die.
>
> (verses 19-20)

He looks *forward* to the unchanging faithfulness of God:

> Of old you laid the foundation of the earth. . .
> They will perish, but you will remain. . .
> but you are the same, and your years have no end.
>
> (verses 25-27)

Once overwhelmed with melancholy and pessimism, filled with uncertainty, and broken by his sense that God's face was hidden from him for ever, he now looks forward, even beyond his own life span, with joyful anticipation and a deep sense of security in the glorious promises of his Lord:

The children of your servants shall dwell *secure*;
their offspring shall be *established* before you.

(verse 28, italics added)

Before we leave this psalm we should note one final thing. Its closing
words (verses 25-27) are quoted in the opening chapter of the Letter
to the Hebrews (see *Heb.* 1:10-12). There they are seen as a description of Christ. 'Your Rock,' wrote Samuel Rutherford to a discouraged Christian friend, 'is Christ, and it is not your Rock which ebbs
and flows, but your sea.'

'Twixt gleams of joy and clouds of doubt
  Our feelings come and go;
Our best estate is tossed about
  In ceaseless ebb and flow.
No mood of feeling, form of thought
  Is constant for a day;
But thou, O Lord, thou changest not;
  The same thou art alway.

I grasp thy strength, make it mine own,
  My heart with peace is blest;
I lose my hold, and then comes down
  Darkness, and cold unrest.
Let me no more my comfort draw
  From my frail hold of thee,
In this alone rejoice with awe
  Thy mighty grasp of me.

 Out of that weak, unquiet drift
  That comes but to depart,
To that pure heaven my spirit lift
  Where thou unchanging art.
Lay hold of me with thy strong grasp,
  Let thy almighty arm
In its embrace my weakness clasp,
  And I shall fear no harm.

Thy purpose of eternal good
  Let me but surely know;
On this I'll lean—let changing mood
  And feeling come or go—
Glad when thy sunshine fills my soul,
  Not lorn when clouds o'ercast,
Since thou within thy sure control
  Of love dost hold me fast.

John Campbell Shairp

Jesus Christ is the same
yesterday and today and forever (*Heb.* 13:8).

. . . .

Can I Be Pure?

Have you failed again? Fallen into sin yet again? Each time gets more discouraging. Most of the time you feel that you have let down your Lord. But do you sometimes wonder whether he may have simply turned away from you and left you to your own failures? Does anyone have words of counsel to help you?

Psalm 119 is for you.

Psalm 119:9-16

[9]How can a young man keep his way pure?
   By guarding it according to your word.
[10]With my whole heart I seek you;
   let me not wander from your commandments!
[11]I have stored up your word in my heart,
   that I might not sin against you.
[12]Blessed are you, O LORD;
   teach me your statutes!
[13]With my lips I declare
   all the rules of your mouth.
[14]In the way of your testimonies I delight
   as much as in all riches.
[15]I will meditate on your precepts
   and fix my eyes on your ways.
[16]I will delight in your statutes;
   I will not forget your word.

We would never dream of giving a long book to someone who was in immediate need of help; a booklet, or small paperback perhaps, but nothing demanding. Psalm 119 seems to neglect that principle in several ways. It is a poem specifically written to give instruction, yet it extends to 176 verses. It even seems to have been written with young people especially in mind (verse 9), and yet it goes on, and on! Closer examination reveals the hidden wisdom of this psalm, however: the psalm is divided into segments of eight verses each. Short chapters! It is a booklet.

Notice too the section headings. There are twenty-two of them, one for each letter of the Hebrew alphabet.

There is an additional feature that could scarcely be reproduced in our English Bibles. But it could not be missed by those who first read the psalm in Hebrew. It has an 'acrostic' form: the verses in each section of the psalm all begin with the letter of the alphabet at the head of the section. Verses 1-8 all begin with the letter *aleph* (a), verses 9-16 with the letter *beth* (b) and so on. Ingenious!

What purpose, other than aesthetic, did the poet have in mind? It is not difficult to guess: he meant his psalm to be learned by heart.

Can you imagine sitting beside a struggling Christian and saying, 'Now, if you will only learn this psalm and take it to heart it will help you tremendously'? Of course not. Neither did the author of Psalm 119. He expected us to memorize it and learn its lessons *before* we actually need them. 'Forewarned is forearmed' is a proverb he would have understood.

That principle cannot be overemphasized. It is one we learn from the life of our Lord. In every situation he faced he was able to draw on the wisdom and guidance of God in Scripture; he had filled his memory with it, grasped its meaning, meditated on its practical significance, and was able to use it as 'the sword of the Spirit' (*Eph.* 6:17) in the heat of the battle.

From what we know in general of Jewish education it is probable that Jesus had memorized entire books of the Old Testament, possibly all of it. He knew and used its contents as easily as a housewife knows her way about her own kitchen, or a pharmacist knows his medicines.

This is a psalm written for the young ('How can a young man keep his way pure?'), but only because the child is father of the man. Moral gains made in early life create strong foundations for later years; losses may be irrecoverable:

> Sow a thought, reap an act;
> Sow an act, reap a character;
> Sow a character, reap a destiny.

This great question, 'How can a . . . man keep his way pure?' is a lifelong issue.

Most of us memorize Psalm 119:9 in this way: 'How can a young man keep his way pure? By guarding it according to your word.' God's Word is seen as the *answer* to the question. It is possible, however, that we are meant to see God's Word as the *cause* of the question: 'How can a young man keep his way pure in order to guard it according to your word?'

Scripture, which teaches us how to overcome sin also shows us the deep-seated nature of sin and exposes its widespread influence in our lives. It will show us how to be free from the terrible burden of sin; yet it must first make that sin burdensome to us in order to do so.

The psalmist knows that burden. He struggles with sin. He knows how easily his heart drifts into sinful thoughts and actions: 'Let me not wander from your commandments!' (verse 10).

He knows his tendency to be drawn away from the Lord by the allure of the world and the flesh: 'Turn my eyes from looking at worthless things' (verse 37).

He knows how easily he is dragged down spiritually: 'Hold me up, that I may be safe' (verse 117).

He knows that his heart is deceitful and he is not yet free from the folly of sin. The last words of the psalm recognize this and express an ongoing sense of need: 'I have gone astray like a lost sheep; seek your servant, for I do not forget your commandments' (verse 176). Robert Murray M'Cheyne, the young Scottish preacher whose brief ministry and deeply consecrated life left an impression that still influences those who read his biography, put it well. He confessed that in his heart there remained the seeds of every known sin.

The psalmist knows, too, the opposition anyone who is committed to a life of purity will encounter. This is one of the most frequently recurring notes in the psalm:

> The insolent utterly deride me,
>> but I do not turn away from your law. . .
> Though the cords of the wicked ensnare me,
>> I do not forget your law. . .
> The insolent smear me with lies,
>> but with my whole heart I keep your precepts. . .
> The insolent have dug pitfalls for me;
>> they do not live according to your law. . .
> The wicked have laid a snare for me,
>> but I do not stray from your precepts.
>
> (verses 51, 61, 69, 85, 110)

When we set our hearts on living for Christ, we will face similar opposition.

A document that is alleged to have come into the possession of a field director of the Security Service in the early 1960s illustrates this in a graphic fashion. It listed a series of objectives of secular atheism to destroy the Christian order of the West without resort to the use of armaments. Some of these were as follows:

> Break down cultural standards of morality by promoting pornography and obscenity in books, magazines, motion pictures, radio and TV.
>
> Eliminate all laws governing obscenity by calling them 'censorship' and 'a violation of free speech and free press.'

Discredit the family as an institution. Encourage promiscuity and easy divorce.

Gain control of key positions in radio, TV and motion pictures.

Present homosexuality, degeneracy, and promiscuity as 'normal, natural and healthy.'

Fifty years later, the plan reads like a prophecy come true.

We would, however, be misled if we thought that all we need to do to protect ourselves from such strategies is to attack those who employ them. It is never enough to attack the enemy outside the city walls when the Trojan Horse is already within the gates. Yes, it is important to expose society's sin; but it is far more important that we learn how to keep our lives pure. It is the inward liaison with impurity that is the real enemy.

How, then, can we be pure? That is the great question. The psalmist gives us principles based on his own experience, which we are meant to work out and apply with the help of the rest of Scripture.

1. Seek God with all your heart

> With my whole heart I seek you;
> let me not wander from your commandments.
>
> (verse 10)

This is not the question of the philosopher ('Is there a God?') but of the believer ('I know you, Lord, but can I get to know you better?'). It is not more information that he desires, but fellowship with God.

The person of God has begun to fill his thoughts. This was simple obedience to what Jesus called the greatest commandment: love God with heart, mind, soul, and strength.

The first principle of purity is to love God with the heart and mind. Great thoughts of God expand the heart to contain the emotions that those thoughts excite. In Scripture this is what marks the difference between holiness and wickedness: 'In the pride of his face the wicked does not seek him [God]; all his thoughts are, "There is no God"' (*Psa.* 10:4).

God's glory is revealed in the entire created order: in the beauty and awesome forces in nature; in the wonder of the animal creation; in the amazing phenomenon of human life. His hand is revealed in history; his word is revealed in Scripture.

God is great, glorious, good, holy, righteous, gracious. But natural, sinful minds resist thoughts about him. Like magnets that share the same polarity, water on a duck's back, seed falling on hardened soil, the natural mind is incapable of giving those thoughts room to take a grip on the whole of life. People capable of intense concentration on everything from crossword puzzles to a televised football game are incapable of even a minute of deliberate concentrated thought about God! 'In all his thoughts there is no room for God' (*Psa.* 10:4 NIV).

By contrast, sinful thoughts—what John calls 'the desires of the flesh and the desires of the eyes and pride in possessions' (*1 John* 2:16)—come easily and naturally to us. We turn them over in our minds for extended periods; we can deliberately focus our attention on them. However, we find it hard to focus our minds on thoughts of God.

This explains why the psalmist knew that he needed to seek God *with all his heart*. He is speaking, of course, as someone who knows and has experienced God's grace; this is not a resolution on his part to do better in order to be justified and accepted by God. He knows he already is. Rather he is saying: 'This is what the grace of God produced in my life to enable me to overcome sin and to grow in personal purity.'

One evidence that my life is Spirit-controlled is a growing ability to think great thoughts about God. For the Spirit enables me to say: 'Seek his face!' and to respond, 'Your face, LORD, I will seek' (*Psa.* 27:8 NIV).

The result of this seeking God is praise for him: 'Blessed are you, O LORD' the psalmist cries out (verse 12); 'In the way of your testimonies I delight as much as in all riches' (verse 14). 'I will delight in your statutes' (verse 16). Thus heaviness of heart gives way to praise, sorrow because of failure gives way to joy, a distaste for sin gives way to a delight in purity.

But how is it that great thoughts of God bring purity?

When God seems great to us and we love to think about his character and the way he has revealed himself, we do not—indeed cannot—simultaneously think about sin. It cannot dwell in his presence. When we set our minds on the revelation of God's glorious character, we breathe in so much spiritual oxygen that sinful thoughts are suffocated; they have no room to develop in our minds.

When we meditate on the attributes of God—on the love of the Father, the grace displayed in Christ the Son, the blessings of communion with the Holy Spirit—we are 'transformed by the renewal of [y]our mind' (*Rom.* 12:2).

Any personal relationship in which there is a 'marriage of true minds' results in people beginning to think like each other. Sometimes they even seem to begin to look like each other! That is the inevitable consequence when we spend so much time with someone else, that even when absent from them we are always thinking about them. Our life reflects the influence of their person.

It should not surprise us that fellowship with God has a similar effect on us, for it is the greatest and most intimate of all our relationships: 'And we all, with unveiled face, beholding [or reflecting] the glory of the Lord, are being transformed into the same image from one degree of glory to another. For this comes from the Lord who is the Spirit' (*2 Cor.* 3:18).

When we meditate on the character of God, as Christians who have seen 'the light of the knowledge of the glory of God in the face of Jesus Christ' (*2 Cor.* 4:6), we see our sin in its true light. We develop a 'taste' for the presence of God's glory, and we lose our 'taste' for sin.

Sin is contrary to the will of God because it is the antithesis of his character. When we sin, we distort lives that were made to reflect his image. When we seek God with our whole hearts, and meditate on his character, the real nature of sin becomes clear to us. At last our eyes are opened!

As we gaze on the beauty of God's holiness, we begin to see our sin in its ugliness; in the light of his faithfulness we see how tawdry is our unfaithfulness; arrested by his grace we recognize the shame of our sin. As we recall that he is unchanging in all of his attributes, we realize that our sin has made us unreliable in all of ours. Knowing him in this way is all the reward sought by the wholeheartedness the psalmist mentions.

Our family vacations used to be taken on the east coast of Scotland. The cold North Sea became the children's swimming pool. But our two eldest boys differed in their attitude to the bitterly cold water. One would go down to the edge, dip a foot in, and shudder. Meanwhile his brother would be rushing down the sand and would run straight into the water until the waves overpowered him and he collapsed into the sea. Moments later he would emerge, shouting to his brother, 'Come on in, it's great!' But his brother felt only the cold, and could not see how exhilarating the water must be.

So it is in the life of faith; wholehearted abandonment to the Lord brings immeasurable joy and freedom. But if I stand on the shoreline of his grace, I will never know the power to overcome sin that wholehearted love and devotion to him produce.

2. Treasure God's Word in Scripture

'I have stored up [hidden (NIV)] your word in my heart,' the psalmist writes, 'that I might not sin against you' (verse 11). The Hebrew term *'imrâ* can be translated appropriately as 'word' or 'promise.' In this context, however, it may mean 'saying.' The psalmist has carefully learned and meditated on the 'sayings' of God, the specific truths that are taught in Scripture. He has 'hidden' them, not in the sense of obscuring them, but of knowing what and where they are. The teaching of Scripture, what we might call its 'doctrines,' are familiar to him; he knows them and has access to them.

This tells us something very important about his personal Bible study. Many Christians have a tendency to read Scripture each day almost as though it were a divine horoscope. Their only interest is to discover what the passage they are reading 'says' to them 'for today.' Of course there is benefit in that kind of Bible reading, but it is shortlived.

We can easily discover whether we have made that mistake. Perhaps you are reading through Paul's letter to the Ephesians. If you had kept a written record of what you have been learning, would someone else be able to read it and find out what Ephesians teaches? Or would they find themselves reading a spiritual autobiography? Have you read Scripture as though it were only a mirror in which you saw your own reflection? It does have that effect, of course; but its chief function is to reflect God and to teach us about him.

Unless we hide God's Word in our minds and hearts in this way, and come to know the specific teaching of Scripture, we will be under-resourced in our Christian lives. We will lack the specific 'sayings' or teaching that God gives us in Scripture to enable us to resist and overcome sin. Failure here will be bound to discourage us.

But what 'sayings' or teachings do we need to hide in our hearts to help us to overcome sin? We can summarize the most important of them, in the acrostic style of the psalmist: there are Five R's!

1. Remember your new identity in Christ.
The New Testament is constantly reminding us that we are 'in Christ.'

We were born 'in Adam,' under the reign of sin, guilt, death, and Satan. But the Spirit has brought us to living faith. We have been united to Jesus Christ; we are no longer 'in Adam' but 'in Christ.' Our lives no longer depend on, nor are they dominated by, the powers that were let loose in Adam's family; now it is the grace, forgiveness, power, and victory of Christ that we inherit.

In Romans 6 Paul explains one immediate consequence of this: if we are united to Christ, we are united to him in his death to sin.

On the cross Christ entered death's territory and came into sin's dominion. There he destroyed it. He is no longer under its reign. If we are 'in Christ,' we share in what he has done. So Paul says that in him we have become the kind of people 'who died to sin' (see *Rom.* 6:2).

Remember the kind of person you are. You are no longer a prisoner under sin's dominion; you are free. You are no longer paralyzed, sinning inevitably. In Christ you belong to another kingdom altogether, in which grace reigns through righteousness (see *Rom.* 5:21). There is hope! You do not need to be defeated by sin anymore.

2. Recognize the difference between 'reigning sin' and 'remaining sin.'
Before we became Christians we were under the reign of sin. Now Christ reigns over our lives and in our hearts and sin no longer reigns (see *Rom.* 5:21; 6:14). But that does not mean that sin no longer dwells in our hearts, for the Bible distinguishes between: the overthrow of the reign of sin, and the destruction of the presence of sin. Sin's reign over you ended when you were united to Christ, yet its presence in you will not be abolished until glory.

It is very easy to confuse these two things. We sin and are tempted to conclude, 'There I go; sin reigns again.' We feel paralyzed; failure seems inevitable, and we despair. But we have confused the continuing presence of sin with the reign of sin. Understand the distinction and we realize that losing one skirmish is not the loss of the war.

3. Realize what your responsibilities are.

Paul sums up a great deal of his teaching in two starkly contrasting statements about his Christian life:

'Sin. . . dwells within me' (*Rom.* 7:17), yet 'Christ. . . lives in me' (*Gal.* 2:20).

So long as both these things are true, my life is bound to be a battleground between Christ as Lord of my life and the presence of sin, demanding its rights as a 'squatter' in my soul. If Christ is Master, however, my responsibility is clear: sin must be evicted.

There can be no half measures here. That is why the language of the New Testament is so radical: if your right hand or eye leads you to yield to sin, says Jesus, cut it off, pluck it out (see *Matt.* 5:29-30). Paul echoes his Master's teaching. Since you belong to Christ and have been given new life in him, 'put to death' the sinful tendencies and urges that remain (*Rom.* 8:13; *Col.* 3:5).

What does that mean in practical terms? If we want to keep our way pure, we will make it a principle in our lives not to go where our shoes can pick up dirt. We cannot avoid living in the world; we must daily live in the context of its impurities, but we do not need to share them. 'You cannot stop the birds of the air flying around your head,' said Luther, 'but you can prevent them making their nest in your hair!'

God is well able to sanctify us through his truth and to keep us in this world, as Jesus prayed (see *John* 17:15, 17). But that prayer is answered by our active progress in holiness. It is our responsibility to 'pluck out,' to 'cut off,' and to 'mortify.' That will mean guarding our minds and what we allow them to dwell on, our eyes and what we look at, our feet and where we go, our hands and what we touch. Christian purity involves our bodies as well as our minds:

> I appeal to you. . . by the mercies of God, to present your bodies as a living sacrifice. . . be transformed by the renewal of your mind.
>
> (*Rom.* 12:1-2)

4. Resist sinful tendencies immediately when you notice them.

That hurts. It hurts to say no to ourselves. It may 'hurt' us in our relationships with others to do so. But we must learn how slight those hurts are by comparison with the hurt that sin does to our fellowship with God.

It 'hurt' Joseph to resist the sexual advances of Potiphar's wife. It cost him his freedom. But he knew his identity as a child of God. His privileges had taken hold of and mastered him: 'How then can I do this great wickedness and sin against God?' (*Gen.* 39:9). He is not denying his ability to sin, but stressing the inconsistency, the incongruity of it for someone in his position.

We must similarly learn our identity in Christ until that response is instinctive in us too. We shall not be the losers any more than Joseph was. Had he not been faithful, he would not have ended up in prison; but had he never been in prison, he would never have become prime minister of Egypt! Faithful in little (Potiphar's house, *Gen.* 39:9) he was given responsibility for much (all Egypt! *Gen.* 41:39-41).

It would have 'hurt' David to refuse the desires that rose in him as he strolled on his rooftop one spring evening and caught sight of the beautiful Bathsheba bathing (*2 Sam.* 11).

David should have returned to his rooms and asked the Lord to quench the fiery dart of temptation that had found its mark in his emotions. He should have reminded himself who he was: servant of the Lord, anointed King of Israel, prophet of the Most High God. He had killed a giant with a pebble when he had been 'strong in the Lord and in the strength of his might' (*Eph.* 6:10). Now, sadly, he was conquered by late-night temptation. He forgot himself—in every conceivable sense.

> Sin rather than 'twill out of action be,
> Will pray to stay, though but a while with thee.
> One night, one hour, one moment, will it cry;
> Embrace me in thy bosom else I die;
> Time to repent [saith it] I will allow,

And help, if to repent thou knowest not how.
But if you give it entrance at the door,
 It will come in, and may go out no more [italics added].

John Bunyan

Grace, says Paul, teaches us to say 'no':

> For the grace of God has appeared. . . training us to renounce ungodliness and worldly passions, and to live self-controlled, upright and godly lives in this present age. . .
>
> (*Titus* 2:11-12)

5. Replace all rejected sin with its opposite: grace.

When we hear Paul speak about 'mortification of sin' (*Rom.* 8:13; *Col.* 3:5) it conjures up pictures of medieval monks flaying themselves physically and denying themselves every pleasant experience, in order to be pure. The great mistake they made was not simply that they were negative in the wrong ways; they also failed to be positive in the right ways.

When Scripture urges us to lay aside the impurities in our lives, it simultaneously urges us to develop new graces. All our efforts to deal with our anger will come to nothing if we do not develop patience. Lust will not lie down unless we develop Spirit-given love that allows lust no air to breathe in our lives.

Paul expresses this principle very clearly to the Colossians. 'You are no longer the old men and women you were, in Adam,' he argues; 'you are new men and women in Christ (see *Col.* 3:9-10). Well, then, dress appropriately!'

> Put to death therefore what is earthly in you: sexual immorality, impurity, passion, evil desire, and covetousness, which is idolatry. . . In these you once walked, when you were living in them. But now you must put them all away: anger, wrath, malice, slander, and obscene talk from your mouth. Do not lie to one another, *seeing that you have put off the old self with its practices and have put on the new self, which is being renewed in knowledge after the image of its creator. . .* Put on then, *as God's chosen ones, holy and beloved,* compassion, kindness, humility,

meekness, and patience, bearing with one another and, if one has a complaint against another, forgiving each other, as the Lord has forgiven you. . . Let the word of Christ dwell in you richly. . .

(*Col.* 3:5, 7-10,12-13,16, italics added)

This is what it means to say: 'Lord, I have been so depressed by my sin and failure in the Christian life. But now I want to let the word of Christ dwell in me richly. *"I have stored up your word in my heart, that I might not sin against you."'*

....

10

Learning Contentment

It has been said, cleverly yet wisely, that the shortest psalms sometimes take the longest to learn. That is certainly true of Psalm 131.

> ### Psalm 131
>
> [1]O LORD, my heart is not lifted up;
>   my eyes are not raised too high;
> I do not occupy myself with things
>   too great and too marvellous for me.
> [2]But I have calmed and quietened my soul,
>   like a weaned child with its mother;
>   like a weaned child is my soul within me.
> [3]O Israel, hope in the LORD
>   from this time forth and for evermore.

If we were to give it a title, we could do worse than the one used by the Puritan Jeremiah Burroughs for his book on this theme: *The Rare Jewel of Christian Contentment.*

Burroughs was right to call contentment a 'jewel,' because it is beautiful to see this grace in a person's life; it sweetens the spirit of those who are younger; it lends dignity to those who are older and helps us to understand what the psalmist meant when he said that the Lord 'beautifies the meek with salvation' (*Psa.* 149:4 KJV).

But he was also, sadly, on target when he described contentment as a 'rare' jewel. It is certainly all too rare in our own acquisitive age, when Christian people too can easily be swept along in the spirit of discontent that surrounds them.

Perhaps we have lost the ability that earlier Christians had to discern the difference between being contented *with* the world (which we can never be) and being contented *in* the world (which by God's grace we should be).

All too often we allow situations and circumstances that are less than ideal, or even wrong, to destroy our contentment. We realize too little what a sad and ugly thing it is when a child of God expresses discontent that is really rooted in a deep discontent with God. Yet nothing should more clearly mark his children than a sweet spirit of contentment. They alone possess 'solid joys and lasting treasure' (John Newton); they alone can sing with Isaac Watts that

> The men of grace have found
> Glory begun below;

> The hill of Zion yields
> A thousand sacred sweets,
> *Before* we reach the heavenly fields,
> Or walk the golden streets [italics added].

It is significant that Psalm 131, the song of the contented, is located in the Psalter toward the end of a collection of fifteen psalms (120-134) that all have the same title: 'A song of ascents.' This title is a little mysterious and requires some explanation.

I recently participated in a conference in which each participant received a conference brochure in their registration pack. Inside the brochure was not only the programme but also the words of all the hymns and songs to be used in the worship of the weekend.

These psalms were probably first brought together for a similar purpose. The 'ascent' referred to in the title is almost certainly the geographical ascent made by pilgrims coming to Jerusalem for the great Old Testament festivals.

The fifteen psalms may not be listed in any strict order of singing, but, like most hymnbooks, there does seem to be a certain progression in them. It is not surprising that some students have even wondered whether the 'ascent' in the titles includes the idea of an ascent in spiritual experience.

Psalm 121, for example, would be very appropriate for the beginning of a pilgrimage. A novice pilgrim gazes on the hills and mountains he will have to cross in order to get to Jerusalem. The road is hazardous; there are dangers in the day and in the night. Does he have the courage? Will he go? He puts his trust in the Lord from whom help comes, and he receives encouragement from a fellow pilgrim who has gone this way before and known the Lord's hand protecting him (see *Psa.* 121:3-4). He ventures forth.

Soon the pilgrim is in Jerusalem, rejoicing with those who first issued the invitation to him, 'Let us go to the house of the Lord' (*Psa.* 122:1).

The general order continues in the experiences described in the psalms that follow. Praise and worship, fellowship and ministry characterize them. Yet a heightened sense of God's presence has a way of creating a deep, almost overwhelming realization of personal sinfulness. And so Psalm 130 helps the pilgrim to confess his guilt and to rediscover that 'with you there is forgiveness' (*Psa.* 130:4). What a relief to experience at a new level that 'with the Lord there is steadfast love, and with him is plentiful redemption' (*Psa.* 130:7).

This psalm of contentment follows.

Contentment appears to be a simple grace, some might even think it should be easily attained—at least by others! But the compilers of this collection of hymns were shrewder by far; spiritual contentment, contentment with God, they understood, is a fruit manifested only by those in whom God's grace has been deeply rooted.

But what is contentment? It is easier to applaud it than to define it. It is the philosopher's stone, says the proverb, that turns all it touches into gold. But what is it?

Contentment

The psalmist also found it easier to describe and illustrate content-ment than to define it:

> But I have calmed and quieted my soul,
>   like a weaned child with its mother;
>   like a weaned child is my soul within me.

(verse 2)

A vivid picture! He is like a child weaned from his familiar diet of his mother's milk. He is now content to have a regular diet of solid food. This is how it is between the psalmist's soul and God. He rests in God's will. He trusts in his wisdom; he is contented with whatever God provides and purposes.

Yet, no doubt intentionally, this picture suggests the calm after the storm. For some mothers the mental and emotional effort involved in weaning their children is one of the great early dramas of the first years of motherhood. It is a conflict situation. The memory it con-jures up is one of fretfulness, tears, even despair! Weaning can be a major battle of wills between mother and child. Contentment with solid food is not always easily won.

That is as true spiritually as it is physically, *because the contentment described here is spiritual rather than natural.*

Some of us are more naturally contented than others. We have different tolerance levels in most areas of our lives. If you came into my study, you might say, 'I don't know how you can possibly work in this chaos!' But, then, I might find your work space uncomfortably orderly! Similarly, you may go into a friend's kitchen and wonder how she can endure it; it is so small, so poorly equipped—yet she is such an infuriatingly relaxed and good cook! You, by contrast, cannot even begin to prepare a meal until everything is set neatly in order, yet you fret and worry over cooking for your guests. We are tempera-mentally very different.

But this psalm is not speaking about that kind of natural content or discontent which is dependent on our background, our upbringing, and our native personality. We are not born with the contentment of which the Bible speaks; it does not come from our upbringing. We have to learn it: 'I have *learned* in whatever situation I am to be content,' says Paul (*Phil.* 4:11). He implies that his contentment was the result of the many learning experiences of his Christian life. He was certainly not a naturally contented individual.

The illustration of the weaned child learning contentment seems all the more vivid when we remember that Jewish mothers in Old Testament times weaned their children much later than we do—sometimes they were four or even five years old. Can you imagine coping with a four-year-old under those circumstances? What potential for conflict!

But this is the point. Contentment means being at ease with God's provision for our lives. That, however, does not come easily to us. It may come only after prolonged battles between our own will for our lives and the will of our Heavenly Father.

Spiritual contentment is rooted in and based on an inward relationship to God, not on external circumstances.

Consider Paul's words to his Philippian friends about learning to be content. They were written from prison, probably in Rome. Deprived of his ordinary liberty, his contentment could not have been the result of his external circumstances. How then was it nourished? Because it was rooted in considerations that transcend physical and material circumstances: 'I can do all things through him who strengthens me' (*Phil.* 4:13) was his own explanation.

How easy for the apostle to pray: 'Lord, I realize that I have been discontented with your ways with me in the past. But if you will only get me out of this prison I will be content.'

We at least think that way: 'Lord, if only I had this, or lived there, or had that gift, or a little more money, or… then I would be content.' But that is not contentment-minus-some-small-details; it is discontentment. It may even be covetousness.

True contentment is not the same thing as getting whatever we want; it is submitting to the Lord's will and learning to desire what he does. Only then will we discover that his will is good, perfect, and acceptable (*Rom.* 12:2).

The unweaned child prefers his mother's milk and the comfort of the accustomed. But the mother knows what the child needs and is determined to give that, however fraught with conflict the weaning process turns out to be. The mother knows best. When we are weaned as infants, we lose the milk we desire in order to receive the solid food we need. Milk satisfies the child; but it will not satisfy the mother.

So too in the world of the spirit: the weaning that brings us to contentment in the Lord takes place through loss. Every experience in life in which we are deprived of what we naturally want becomes the means by which our Father gives us what he knows we really need.

That is true of the most severe losses in life, as the hymn writer Horatius Bonar saw:

> Dear ones are leaving, and as they depart
> Make room within for someone yet more dear.

But it is also true of every loss or pain, small or great, as John Newton teaches us in his poem 'Prayer answered by crosses':

> I asked the Lord that I might grow
>   In faith and prayer and every grace,
> Might more of his salvation know,
>   And seek more earnestly his face.
>
> 'Twas He who taught me thus to pray,
>   And He, I trust, has answered prayer;
> But it has been in such a way
>   As almost drove me to despair.

I hop'd that in some favour'd hour
    At once He'd answer my request
And by his love's constraining power,
    Subdue my sins, and give me rest.

Instead of this, He made me feel
    The hidden evils of my heart,
And bade the angry powers of hell
    Assault my soul in every part.

Yea, more, with His own hand He seemed
    Intent to aggravate my woe,
Crossed all the fair designs I schemed,
    Blasted my gourds, and laid me low.

'Lord, why is this?' I trembling cried,
    'Wilt Thou pursue Thy worm to death?'
'Tis in this way,' the Lord replied,
    'I answer prayer for grace and faith.

'These inward trials I employ,
    From self and pride to set thee free
And break thy schemes of earthly joy,
    That thou mayest seek thine all in Me.'

When Christ is all, that is contentment. Of course, when we first come to Christ, we yield our all to him. But that radical consecration expresses itself in an ongoing way. As we have more of life to yield, so we are summoned to go on seeking our all in Christ, holding lightly all that we have and are. This is contentment. But how is it learned?

The School of Contentment

There are two errors often made in thinking about spiritual progress. The first is to think that it is our own accomplishment; by contrast, the second is to think that it takes place without engaging our own mind, will, and affections.

Paul learned contentment; but for him such learning involved the ministry of God's Spirit engaging his own activity in the learning process. He had earlier explained the two-fold character of this to the Philippians:

> . . .work out your own salvation with fear and trembling, for it is God who works in you, both to will and to work for his good pleasure.
>
> (*Phil.* 2:12-13)

Contentment is part of this sanctification. God is its author; but the contentment is ours and manifests itself in the way *we* think and feel. God brings us a spirit of contentment; yet that spirit actively rests in his will, submits to his purposes, and is contented with him. The same, we may assume, was true of David. Indeed he says as much:

'I have *calmed and quietened* my soul' (verse 2, italics added). He had fought and won the battle for contentment. But how?

David did two things:

1. *He guarded the ambitions of his heart:*

> O LORD, my heart is not lifted up; my eyes are not raised too high (verse 1).

He no longer assumes that he knows what is best for himself. This is not to say that his ambitions were necessarily wrong. Many of them were excellent in themselves.

There is nothing wrong in aiming high. But David is now concerned that his heart should be set only on what pleases God, and on the purposes which God has for him. He had begun to appreciate a divine logic, which Paul would later underscore: since everything we have, are, or accomplish is because of God's grace, and leaves us nothing to boast about in ourselves, why do we still go on boasting as though these were our own unaided achievements (see *1 Cor.* 4:7)? It is not only illogical, but ugly to do so.

David's life provides a perfect example of what he is talking about here. No doubt, from the moment Samuel had anointed him to be the future king, the seed of godly ambition had been sown in young David's heart. He had been given an intimation of future greatness. The Spirit of the Lord came upon him and his heart was set on gaining the throne (see *1 Sam.* 16:12-13). If it is a noble thing to set one's heart on being an overseer (see *1 Tim.* 3:1), it is surely at least as noble to desire to be king when God has called to that service.

But it is ignoble if that desire puffs us up with self-importance rather than humbles us with a deep sense of privilege. Sadly, that is all too common, even in those God eventually uses.

Joseph seems to have been guilty of pride and discontent when as a teenager he received prophetic intimations of his own future greatness. Instead of being humbled and asking God to keep him for such service, he boasted insensitively to his brothers (see *Gen.* 37:5-11). It was only after many years of discipline, loss, and specific disappointments that Joseph could be trusted with greatness.

Even Moses' usefulness seems to have been crippled at first by similar proud impatience. Stephen explains that when Moses killed an Egyptian who was mistreating an Israelite, he 'supposed that his brothers would understand that God was giving them salvation by his hand, *but they did not understand*' (*Acts* 7:25, italics added). Moses, too, would face many years of patient discipline until he learned to be content as a humble shepherd in the desert. That made him the meek man who was fit for the greatness God gave him (see *Num.* 12:3). Certainly in earlier years he could not have said, 'My heart is not lifted up.' In fact his 'heart' *was* 'raised too high.' It took great loss and disappointment to empty Moses of Moses.

We know of two occasions in David's life when his God-given ambition to be king was put to the test by opportunities to fulfil it before God's time.

Saul pursued David in the Desert of En Gedi and was searching for him in the area known as the Crags of the Wild Goats. The king made a 'comfort stop' and actually entered the very cave where David and his men were in hiding (see *I Sam.* 24)! 'This is obviously the hand of God,' the men said to David. What a way for prophecy seemingly to be fulfilled. The men must have been beside themselves with excitement. Saul could be eliminated.

But David saw that there was something more important than fulfilling his ambitions, even his God-given ambitions: obedience to God's Word. Saul, despite his sin, was still the Lord's anointed. David rebuked his men for their suggestion. He stilled and quieted his soul, rejecting pride by humbly submitting to the clearly revealed moral will of God.

A similar opportunity arose later when David and Abishai crept into Saul's tent under cover of darkness and found Saul asleep. Abishai turned to his leader and said:

'God has given your enemy into your hand this day. Now please let me pin him to the earth with one stroke of the spear, and I will not strike him twice' (*I Sam.* 26:8). Again David refused:

> But David said to Abishai, 'Do not destroy him, for who can put out his hand against the LORD's anointed and be guiltless?' And David said, 'As the LORD lives, the LORD will strike him, or his day will come to die, or he will go down into battle and perish. The LORD forbid that I should put out my hand against the LORD's anointed.'
>
> (*I Sam.* 26:9-11)

David's ambition to be on the throne was held in place by a greater ambition: to yield his whole life to the Lord and to conform to his commandments, whatever the personal cost might be.

Such a man can afford to wait God's purposes coming to their own fulfilment. He does not harbour ambitions that are outside the will of his Lord.

This guiding principle, 'God's will, but in God's way and at God's time,' meant that David was called to die to himself, to trust in God's perfect wisdom and not in his own. Others urged him to take what was surely his 'by right' *now*. David recognized that nothing is ours by right. We are what we are only by God's grace. He knew he could not be God's man any other way. Sadly it was his later abandonment of this principle that led to his spiritual collapse.

'It has always been my ambition,' wrote Robert Murray M'Cheyne, 'to have no plans as regards myself.' Paul's sole ambition was 'that I may know [Christ] and the power of his resurrection, and may share his sufferings, becoming like him in his death, that by any means possible I may attain the resurrection from the dead' (*Phil.* 3:10). That is the only safe way to live.

2. *He controlled the preoccupations of his mind:*

> I do not occupy myself with things too great or too marvellous for me (verse 1).

This is the pathway to contentment.

David deliberately refused to allow his mind to become preoccupied with things that were beyond his possession. While he had a right desire to serve God on the throne of Israel, so long as God had put that throne in the possession of another he refused to be preoccupied with it. It was safe enough in the Lord's hands.

Forget that principle—as David did in relationship to Bathsheba (see *2 Sam.* 11-12)—and we lose our spiritual bearings.

It is all too easy to see this principle illustrated in the lives of those who have plenty and thirst for more. But the same temptation faces those who have little. Jesus warns us that not only 'the deceitfulness of riches' but 'the cares of the world . . . and the desires for other things'—preoccupations, sometimes even obsessions, which the poor as well as the rich experience—can choke the good seed of God's Word in our hearts (see *Mark* 4:18-19).

The lesson is clear. If you would learn contentment, guard the preoccupations of your mind.

David also refused to be preoccupied with 'things too marvellous' for him, things that were beyond his understanding.

His earlier life was a beautiful expression of this. He had been anointed by Samuel, had destroyed Goliath, and proved himself in every way superior to Saul. Why then did he have to suffer? Why did he have to wait for his time to come? What good was God doing when the need for David's leadership grew daily more obvious?

Hunted like a criminal and forced into the company of the outcasts of society, David doubtless found it difficult to understand the wisdom and the love of God. Yet he refused to allow himself to become obsessed with finding an answer to all of his questions. He would trust God's wisdom and wait for God's timing.

Without that discipline of mind we will never know spiritual contentment in a world like this. We are not God, and there is much we must learn to leave in his hands. That would seem to be the logical thing for creatures with frail and fallen understanding to do. More important, it is the biblical thing to do:

> Who among you fears the LORD
>   and obeys the voice of his servant?
> Let him who walks in darkness
>   and has no light
> trust in the name of the LORD
>   and rely on his God.
>   (*Isa.* 50:10)

When we experience pain, disappointment, or tragedy in our lives, the most natural question to ask is 'Why?' Sometimes we find hints of answers in Scripture: through these things God teaches us his grace, disciplines us, equips us the better to serve him, shows us his presence in new ways, and perhaps even allows Satan to test us, as we have seen.

Yet these remain partial answers. For now we see only a pale reflection of God's wisdom; we know and understand only in part. We do not see the whole picture (see *1 Cor.* 13:12). *That is how things are.* We must learn to apply Jesus' words to our lives: 'What I am doing you do not understand now, but afterwards you will understand' (*John* 13:7). Meanwhile, we know that he reigns and that he understands. We can trust his wisdom.

We know we can because he has proved that he works even the deep evil of this world into his overall plan for the blessing of his people.

The cross was the most evil event perpetrated in human history: the Lord of glory was crucified by wicked men. Yet that worst of all deeds was also the wisest and most gracious act of God (see *Acts* 2:23). It is the signal to us that where we cannot understand we can still trust.

This requires a deliberate commitment of the mind. That hurts when our natural instinct is to let our minds and emotions dwell on our pain, loss, and disappointment. But it is a hurt that heals.

Scripture gives us a poignant example of this in the life of Jacob. He experienced a great change when he met with God at Peniel. But some time afterward, Jacob's wife Rachel went into labour as they travelled from Bethel to Bethlehem. She died shortly after childbirth.

Imagine the scene. Jacob, who had wrestled with God and held his ground, watched helplessly as his wife lay dying. Just before she died she turned from gazing at her baby boy to look at her husband: 'Jacob,' she said, 'Call him Ben-Oni.'

That was Rachel's dying wish. 'Call him Son-of-my-sorrow.' 'But,' we are told, 'his father called him Benjamin' (*Gen.* 35:18). Ben-jamin means 'Son-of-my-right-hand.' Jacob would not think of his newborn son as the cause of his grief, but as the recipient of his highest blessing, the blessing of his right hand. He would not allow himself to become preoccupied with a question he could never answer—'Why did God let her die when we needed her most?' By God's grace, even in the midst of tragedy, there would be blessing.

It is impossible to imagine what effort of mind and will it took for Jacob lovingly to decline his wife's dying wish. But he knew he needed to commit himself to the principle that the Lord takes from us one blessing only to prepare us for another.

It is harder to learn contentment than we may have assumed. Perhaps that is why David introduces verse 2 with a Hebrew expression commonly employed in oaths: 'God knows if I have not calmed and quieted my soul.' It is an expression of the strenuousness of the way of grace. But David knew that the God of grace can take every strain we place on him, and so he turned to others as he concluded his brief poem, and urged them:

> O Israel [yes, *Israel!*], hope in the LORD
> from this time forth and for evermore.
>
> (verse 3)

Others in Old Testament days heard him and shared that trust:

> Though the fig tree should not blossom,
>   nor fruit be on the vines,
> the produce of the olive fail
>   and the fields yield no food,
> the flock be cut off from the fold
>   and there be no herd in the stalls,
> yet I will rejoice in the LORD;
>   I will take joy in the God of my salvation.
> God, the LORD, is my strength;
>   he makes my feet like the deer's;
>   he makes me tread on my high places.
>
> (*Hab.* 3:17-19)

Others since have learned to share his childlike trust and commitment:

> And shall I pray thee change thy will, my Father?
> Until it be according unto mine?
> But, no, Lord, no, that never shall be, rather
> I pray thee blend my human will with thine.
> I pray thee hush the hurrying, eager longing,

Learning Contentment

I pray thee soothe the pangs of keen desire;
See in my quiet places wishes thronging.
Forbid them, Lord. Purge though it be with fire.

And work in me to will and do thy pleasure.
Let all within me, peaceful, reconciled,
Tarry content my Wellbeloved's leisure,
At last, at last, even as a weaned child.

Amy Carmichael

Never Deserted

At noon on the day of the crucifixion of Jesus of Nazareth darkness descended on the Holy Land. Three hours later, his loud voice was heard, penetrating that darkness with a question that expressed an even greater sense of darkness. He cried in his native tongue, 'Eloi, Eloi, lema sabachthani?'—'My God, my God, why have you forsaken me?' (*Mark* 15:34).

The words are an exact quotation from the first verse of Psalm 22. Jesus made them his own.

Think about what that means:

> O God, O God, why have you forsaken Jesus?
> Why are you so far from saving him,
> from the words of his groaning?
> O God, he cries by day, but you do not answer, by night,
> but he finds no rest.
> Yet you are holy, enthroned on the praises of Israel.
>
> In you his fathers trusted;
> they trusted and you delivered them.
> To you they cried and were rescued;
> in you they trusted and were not put to shame.
>
> But Jesus is a worm and not a man,
> scorned by mankind and despised by the people.
> All who see him mock him;
> they make mouths at him; they wag their heads:
> 'Jesus trusts in the LORD; let him deliver him.

DESERTED BY GOD?

Let him rescue Jesus,
for he delights in him.'

Yet you are he who took Jesus from the womb;
you made him trust you at my mother's breasts.
On you was he cast from his birth,
and from his mother's womb you have been his God.
Be not far from Jesus, for trouble is near,
and there is none to help.

Many bulls encompass Jesus;
strong bulls of Bashan surround him.
They open wide their mouths at him,
like a ravening and roaring lion.
Jesus is poured out like water,
and all his bones are out of joint;
Jesus' heart is like wax;
it is melted within his breast.
Jesus' strength is dried up like a potsherd,
and his tongue sticks to his jaws;
you lay him in the dust of death.

For dogs encompass Jesus;
a company of evildoers encircles him,
they have pierced his hands and his feet—
Jesus can count all his bones—
they stare and gloat over him.
They divide Jesus' garments among them,
and for his clothing they cast lots.

But you, O LORD, do not be far off!
O you his help, come quickly to his aid!
Deliver his soul from the sword,
his precious life from the power of the dog!
Save Jesus from the mouth of the lion!
You have rescued him from the horns of the wild oxen!

Jesus will tell of your name to his brothers;
in the midst of the congregation he will praise you:
You who fear the LORD, praise him!

All you offspring of Jacob, praise him!
All you offspring of Jacob, glorify him,
and stand in awe of him, all you offspring of Israel!
For he has not despised or abhorred
the affliction of the afflicted,
and he has not hidden his face from Jesus,
but has heard, when he cried to him.

On the cross Jesus did two things.

1. He took our place:

> In my place condemned he stood
> And sealed my pardon with his blood.

He accepted God's judgment on our sin. Sinless, he became sin for us in order that we might be accounted righteous (*2 Cor.* 5:21). He took our guilt that we might receive God's pardon. He sensed himself alienated from God in order that we might be reconciled to him. He felt forsaken by God in order that we might be accepted by him.

2. He also entered into the deepest and darkest depths of human loneliness, isolation, pain, and distress. When Mark records that Jesus 'began to be greatly *distressed* and troubled' (*Mark* 14:33, italics added) he uses language that elsewhere 'describes the confused, restless, half-distracted state, which is produced by physical derangement, or by mental distress, as grief, shame, disappointment.'[1]

Jesus' sinless and sensitive spirit felt the full force of the turning of his Father's face from sin. He plumbed the depths. He tasted the darkness of pain, opposition, rejection, loneliness. He comes to us as the Crucified One, who is qualified to understand us and sympathize with us. But he comes also as the Risen One who is able to hold us up and keep us. In him there is comfort. In him there is also security. Come to him if you are weary and burdened. He will give you rest. He has promised.

---

[1] J. B. Lightfoot, *St. Paul's Epistle to the Philippians*, (London: 1913), p. 123.

From you comes the theme of Jesus' praise in the great
    assembly;
    before those who fear you he will fulfil his vows.
The poor will eat and be satisfied;
    they who seek the LORD will praise him—
may your hearts live for ever!
    All the ends of the earth
will remember and turn to the LORD,
    and all the families of the nations
will bow down before him,
    for dominion belongs to the LORD
and he rules over the nations.

All the rich of the earth will feast and worship;
    all who go down to the dust will kneel before him—
    those who cannot keep themselves alive.
Posterity will serve him;
    future generations will be told about the LORD.
They will proclaim his righteousness
    to a people yet unborn—
for he has done it.

Trust him. He will do it.

Also available from
The Banner of Truth Trust

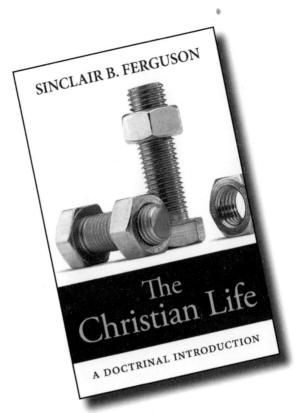

The Christian Life:
A Doctrinal Introduction

Sinclair B. Ferguson

Widely used and appreciated since its first appearance in 1981, this book not only expounds the teaching of Scripture, but outlines its meaning for practical Christian living. It is, as J. I. Packer writes in his preface, theology that is '*practical*, applying Bible teaching with insight and wisdom to the condition of plain people. Christian beginners will get the benefit and the Lord's older sheep, grown tough and stringy maybe, will find themselves edified and perhaps tenderised too'.

ISBN 978 1 84871 259 1   216pp.   paperback